Other Books by Martin P. Mandalu

*The Hidden Wealth of Tanzania

*Tasnia ya Muziki: Mkombozi wa Vijana

* "40 Visites au Saint Sacrement"
Translation: Tafakari 40 za Yesu wa Ekaristi

* "Mission to the Great Lakes"
Translation: Mitume wa Bwana katika Maziwa Makuu

HOW TO THINK AS UNIVERSITY STUDENT

Martin P. Mandalu, PhD

Stella Maris Mtwara University College

How to Think As University Student

© 2020 **Martin P. Mandalu**

All rights reserved

ISBN: 978-9987-9123-6-0

The cover is designed by **Peter Joseph Augustino**

Contact
mpmandalu@gmail.com
+255767864379

Recommended Citation

Mandalu, M.P. 2020. *How to Think As University Student*, Hidden Wealth, Mtwara

Acknowledgement

I am grateful to the creator of all things: visible and invisible for the gift of life through which I am able to explore different talents in me and reveal them to others in the World. I am very much indebted to my beloved wife Namangi and to our sons Alexander and Aaron for understanding and allowing me to steal from them our family time when I researched and worked for this work; without their courage and support, it would have been impossible for me to accomplish it.

Academic and such kind of non-fiction work is built on ideas of previous works by other authors; in that sense, I thank so much the many authors whose works were consulted to come up with this piece. Today we can author all kinds of work because we stand on the shoulders of giants who saw the horizon and beyond before us. Thanks to Professor Hofisi Costa who despite his fixed schedule accepted to write this informative and educative foreword to serve well readers

I am greatly indebted to colleagues and friends who read the manuscript of this work tirelessly; I appreciate all your invaluable help to realise this piece of work. Thus, in appreciation I share all the success with you who assisted me, and I take full responsibility of all the shortcomings encountered in this work.

Dedication

Alexander, Aaron,

Mandalu and Salawa

Foreword

This book closes the gap left by extant literature in the quest for equipping university graduates for employment by concisely examining the soft skills which university graduates must possess for them to be employable. The contemporary relevance of this book cannot be overemphasized since there is a plethora of graduates from various universities across the World who are struggling to secure employment.

This work by Martin P. Mandalu demonstrates his appreciation of the significance of first, independent thinking, which emphasises on originality of thought and ability of individual to demonstrate rationality, neutrality and objectivity in thought process related to individual, organisational and societal affairs.

Second, logical thinking, which zeroes in on thinking effectively, analysis, argumentation and communication and clarity. Third, critical thinking, which stresses on observation, analysis, reflection, evaluation, inference, explanation, problem solving, etcetera.

Fourth, strategic thinking, which concerns with setting a vision and harnessing resources towards the realisation of that vision. This skill highlighted by the author is critical in the sense that there is no individual who can achieve anything in life without envisioning what that achievement is from the beginning. It is also the reason why organisations fail because in the absence of a vision there can never be a meaningful strategy.

Fifth, creative thinking, this skill emphasises on creativity in reflection at issues and problem solving. The author correctly opines that creativity also entails creation of one's self as an individual and envisioning a brighter future by taking advantage of existing opportunities.

Sixth, positive thinking which is a stress management skill critical in improving mental health, better physical and emotional well-being, better life expectancy, as well as coping skills. Here, again the author highlights a vital skill which explains why a lot of graduates may fail in life if they lack emotional wellbeing. Lastly, thinking in systems which empowers one with holistic problem examination skills and perception of a situation as a whole and examining interrelated elements of the system.

The author's succinctly argues that the above mentioned skills are sine qua non for the success of university students and graduates

Costa Hofisi
Professor of Public Administration
Northwest University

Preface

How to Think As University Student aims at impacting University students and all learned fellows positively. It intends to ignite in them the spirit of exploration, development of their hidden potential, and assist their correct thinking as intellectuals.

The book has been inspired by findings of various academic and professional researches on issues related to graduates and employment opportunities. The reviewed literature investigated on graduates in East Africa specifically in Kenya, Tanzania and Uganda; Western Africa in Nigeria and Southern African in South Africa. The findings revealed that many graduates failed to secure employment opportunities because they lacked important skills despite their university education. The increase in unemployment levels in sub-Sahara Africa is caused by various reasons including a severe lack of vital soft skills that are not taught at school.

The book recounts the mission, raison d'être and purpose of establishing universities. It details the evolution of the tertiary level of education in Europe, America and Africa. It analyses the efficiency of skills transmitted to graduates in European and American universities. The chapter proposes African universities adopt and adapt the pragmatic American university model. Since many universities in the world do not teach necessary soft skills to students, this oeuvre proposes the learning of several skills which facilitate self-knowledge, one's value and thirst to live a fulfilled life.

Self-knowledge is the mother of all life skills. It enables an individual know for sure who s/he is and what s/he is not. Through practical means and experiences from other individuals who have succeeded in their paths; you can be able to succeed in yours too. Self-knowledge opens to you the ocean of possibilities as you come to know yourself better and fully.

Moreover, the book proposes the learning of necessary thinking tools. The seven soft skills that you need them in everyday life are independent thinking, logical thinking, critical thinking, strategic thinking, creative thinking, positive thinking and thinking in systems.

Independent thinking occurs when you produce own original thoughts after doing your mental assignment in the mind. It is the ability of an individual to be able to think on their own and present their thoughts before others. Independent thinking is the capacity to employ rationality, neutral and objective view on all issues concerning spheres of life: social problems, organizational affaires, team work affairs and individual problems. The book suggests means that you could use to improve your ability to acquire the skill.

Logic is a skill enabling you to think effectively, analyze, argue and communicate systematically, clearly and make sense. It is a skill that informs all other disciplines and our daily life. Logic is a necessary skill but not taught in many countries in the world; the book suggests methods you can use to acquire or improve your logic skills.

Critical Thinking is another skill discussed extensively which enables a person to think clearly and rationally while understanding the logical connection between ideas. It is a skill involving several other skills specifically reflective and independent thinking. Critical thinking aims at attaining the best possible outcome in any argument. It is also regarded as the ability to analyze information objectively and make reasoned judgment and decisions. In order to do so; it collects and assesses information from many different sources. The book proposes a path that you may use to sharpen your critical thinking skills so that you become more effective in this and related areas.

Strategy is the skill that enables you to examine the current situation, organize the resources around and be able to move to the future with those resources. Moreover, strategy could be taken as the ability to move from where you are to where you want to be; smart strategy is the shortest route to desirable ends with available means.

Creative thinking is yet another skill discussed in the book; the book presents it as the ability to reflect, look at issues differently, and be able to find new ways of solving problems. Moreover, creative thinking is not a professional activity but rather creative thinking is about creating yourself, creating a much better future and taking opportunities that right now you are missing them. How can you do that? The book presents you the steps you can take to become a creative thinker.

Positive thinking is a mental attitude in which an individual anticipates hopes or waits for good things to happen to him/her. A positive mind hopes for happiness, health and happy ending in all undertakings. Positive thinking means approaching life tasks with a positive approach. It does not mean avoiding bad things, rather it extracts good sides of things even in bad situations, looking at the best sides of other individuals, and seeing yourself and your capabilities in a positive attitude. This work provides the means through which you can train your mind to be more positive and benefit from that kind of thinking.

Thinking in systems is an investigative tool for examining problems more completely and accurately before acting. It empowers us with better questions before making conclusions. It starts with observation of collected data to identify patterns of behavior accrued overtime revealing to us the underlying structures that determine the data and pattern. By understanding and changing structures that do not operate well, we can increase choices and create more fulfilling, long-term solutions to chronic problems. Thinking in systems demands you to possess certain qualities: curiosity, kindness, clarity, choice and courage. Thinking in systems involves the readiness to view a situation as a whole, to realize that we are interrelated, to admit that there are multiple interventions to problems

Purpose of life is the reason of you being alive; it is the essence of being in existence for you. It is the raison d'*être* of you being in the world. It is that which you need to do. That means each and every human person including you is here on earth for a specific purpose. Every individual is unique and thus his/her raison d'*être* is also unique different from everybody else's. The task before you is to know what your purpose in life is. Even as you are breathing right now within you there is a purpose for you being alive; you may or may not know about it, all the same there is still a purpose for you being there. What is that purpose? That is your life time task which if you want to live a meaningful life then you should know and live it before you die.

I hope the pages of this book will be useful and help you cultivate the skills that you are short of and create those that you completely lack while they are needed to helping you attain happiness in life. I wish you the best of luck and enjoy the reading.

Martin P. Mandalu
Mitengo, Mtwara

Table of Contents

CHAPTER ONE

Graduates and Employment

Why Were Universities Established?
A university is a catalyst of independent thinking

It is important we begin this journey with a historical perspective of universities. In this part we limit ourselves only to the modern western universities; as older universities were found in Africa; those ones are not part of the subject of this discussion for now.

The conventional definition states a University as an institution of higher education comprising of several fields of studies: arts, science, graduate and professional schools and has the authority to confer certificates, diploma and degrees. It is differentiated from a college by its broader curriculum and the offering of graduate and professional degrees[1]. Moreover, the old modern institutions were also defined by a gathering of students (learners) and masters (dispensers of knowledge)

The modern Western universities that we take as models emerged from the medieval schools known as *studia generalia* which received students from different parts of Europe. These medieval schools had the purpose of educating clerks and monks to a level superior to the Cathedral and monastic school. The first true university in the West was founded at Bologna, Italy in the 11th century specifically in 1088 for the purpose of training students in canon and civil laws. It was followed by the university of Paris (between 1150 and 1170), university of Oxford in the end of 12th century[2]. They received their charters from popes, emperors and kings. Universities were free to govern themselves,

---

[1] https://www.britanica.com/topic/university
[2] De ridder-Symoens, 2003

provided they did not teach atheism or heresy. Independent universities had to finance themselves and so teaching charged fees, and to assure themselves of a decent livelihood they had to please their students[3] which means they could be obliged to favour their students so long as they paid them well.

With time and more especially from the 13th century more universities were established in major cities of Europe. For about five centuries, which is up until the 18th century, most Western universities based their curriculum on seven arts courses: logic, rhetoric, grammar, arithmetic, astronomy, music and geometry.

The 18th century universities taught their students what today we may call foundational courses; the courses indeed formed a concrete foundation which could be likened with that of a story building ready to receive several stories above it; the liberal art. The courses included: logic, grammar, rhetoric, arithmetic, astronomy, music and geometry.

Grammar is an art of putting the right word at the right place. The teaching of grammar to university students intended to help them possess the mastery of language. The mastery of language enables you to express your feelings, your experience, and your abilities in words and in the correct way. This calls you as a university student to learn and master grammar for correct expression of your knowledge. You may possess great connaissance which will need to be expressed correctly for you to share your knowledge and be well understood.

Logic is the science of reasoning; it is a systematic, sensible arrangement of ideas and thoughts, the science of thought. Logic enables you express your thoughts in the correct ways. Ideas, thoughts are the beginning of all your undertaking in life be it engineering, insights, artistic oeuvres and all your plans need to be expressed grammatically and in the logical way for you to make sense before your customers. Such skills or tools align ideas in a systematic and acceptable way.

---

[3] https://www.britanica.com/topic/university

Rhetoric is the art of effective persuasive, convincing speaking and /or writing by using specialized techniques. This tool which is equipped by grammar, logic and other liberal artistic skills enable you sell your ideas and thoughts to the customers. However, you need to be careful about this tool because conventional wisdom reveals rhetoric as a tool enabling speakers win over people even when their speech lacks content. At the time of Socrates, rhetoric was taught by Sophists: teachers who were interested in their students winning debate arguments regardless of the content. What I am saying here is that as much as you put emphasis on becoming a rhetoric leader, you should also learn to acquire content; be a rhetoric leader with content too such as Julius Nyerere (1922-1999), Thomas Sankara (1949-1987), Nelson Mandela (1918-2013) etc

Arithmetic as you may know it, is a branch of mathematics that involves numbers and their properties; the tradition and most important operations of addition, subtraction, multiplication and division. This is more or less the same as basic applied mathematics for our college and/or high school. This was important as it empowered scholars with mathematical thinking; and gave them the skills of solving problems. You need this skill today as you could have your small enterprise that arithmetic skill should be of importance to the operations of your undertaking.

Astronomy is a branch of science dealing with celestial objects phenomena and noumena. It employs some science disciplines such as mathematics, physics and chemistry as it explores the nature, origin and evolution of those objects and phenomena. Those dealing with the discipline are called astronomers. Examples of outstanding astronomers in history that contributed greatly to scientific revolution in the 17th century include: Nicolaus Copernicus (1473-1543) and Johannes Kepler (1571-1630) to mention but just a few.

Music is an art and cultural activity found in all cultures of the world. Its medium is sound organized in time. It contains a number of elements/ components depending on its genre; pitch rhythm, dynamics, timbre and texture. The medieval schools should have borrowed/ adopted this from the Greeks who regarded a human person from the duality point of view: body and soul. The two components had their requirements; the body needed training; gymnasium, and the soul needed music.

Geometry as arithmetic is a branch of mathematics. While arithmetic deals with numbers and their properties; geometry on its part deals with shape, size, relative position of figures, and the properties of space. There are different shapes as we know in mathematics such as the common ones triangle, square, rectangle, trapezium, octagon, hexagon etc

The seven fundamental disciplines taught during the medieval universities to all students contained what you may call in nutrition, balanced diet as it contained necessary intellectual nutrients before one joined a specialized discipline that would normally be their career.

From the art courses which were a foundation to all university students then they proceeded to the profession of their choice based on theology, law and medicine. During that time most universities were influenced by the Roman Catholic teachings and when the church reformation came in (1517-1648), universities defended their faiths; there were those that defended the correct catholic faith and those that defended the correct teaching of Protestantism.

The first modern university in Europe was founded in the 17th century precisely in 1694 by Lutherans; the University of Halle. Halle was the first university to reject religious conservatism in preference to rational and objective intellectual studies, and this was the first place where lectures were conducted in a local language; German, instead of Latin. The innovation of the University of Halle were picked up by Gottingen University founded in 1737 and followed later on by most German and many American universities.

By 18th and 19th centuries religion was slowly but surely replaced as the major power house in the European universities. The change became possible as the curriculum, administration, learning and research became more secularized. The new trend was observed through the University of Berlin, founded in 1809, where by laboratory experiments replaced theological and philosophical speculations as for the other disciplines; they were investigated more objectively and it was, at the same, the University that the modern academic freedom[4] in universities was born. The system of German universities which included advanced research and experimentation in their curriculum influenced other universities worldwide (Pelikan, 1992; Deridder, 2003).

From the 19th century most European universities were secularized and mostly they became funded by states. For gender parity, it was only in the second half of the century that women began to be admitted for studies. At the same time, universities' curricula continued to change. Modern international languages and literature were added; thus, in most cases replacing traditional study of Latin, Greek and Theology. The natural science disciplines as we know them today: biology, chemistry, physics, and engineering became officially recognized in the universities' curricula. And the disciplines that seem to have a great impact to the world today in my views are those that govern the world today: political science, economics, psychology, and sociology started being taught systematically only early 20th century (Pelikan, 1992; Deridder, 2003).

It was only in the 19th century that modern African universities were established as the list below tells it all: Fourah Bay College (1827), Freetown in Sierra Leone; University of Cape Town (1829) South

---

[4] Normally academics in University have great academic freedom when discussing matters of great importance to students or among fellow academics. This freedom is necessary as it is from such discussions of think tanks that communities, countries and the world in general receive new constructive ideas. However, some academics sell their freedom to please some politicians – that is not health for the country for it does not help in creating independent thinkers – university academics are viewed as role models by their students and so they have to be careful about that.

Africa; University of Liberia (1862), Monrovia; University of Khartoum (1902); Stellenbosch University 1903, in South Africa; Cairo University 1908; University of Algiers 1909; University of Fort Hare (1916), South Africa; American University in Cairo 1919; and Makerere University in 1922.

Most of these universities were founded by colonial masters; colonialists founded these universities so as to implant skills to the local population who in turn would work efficiently for their colonial masters. Some of these universities started as schools and later on developed into universities, some of them were developed by missionaries as they taught the word of God; they also introduced some social services such as health care facilities and education such as the University of Fort Hare that was established by missionaries.

These early modern African universities' expansion depended on the needs of the time. The case of the University of Cape Town was typical of this case; it expanded as it stretched to meet the demand of skilled personnel who were needed in the country's newly discovered diamond and gold mining industry in South Africa[5]. The Makerere University started with 14 students who were taught skills that were needed then – they were taught carpentry, building and mechanics[6]. The University of Fort Hare which was established by missionaries in 1916 with both white and black students had purposes of meeting needs of the European colonizers; this purpose of the masters, though not stated explicitly could be witnessed by the Eurocentric curriculum[7].

The aspect of the purpose founding universities in Africa is of great essential to modern economies in the continent as they engage with other economies of the world. We have seen from the above cases and this we may take as the case for most universities in the continent. Universities were established in Africa to train people of a given region, country with specific skills needed to prosper economies of the

---

[5] https://www.uct.ac.za/main/about/history
[6] https://www.mak.ac.ug/about-makerere/historical-background
[7] https://www.ufh.ac.za/About/Pages/History.aspx

founders. This fact is essential for you, as a University student, to know why you joined the University where you are studying now. It is necessary for you to know the purpose / mission of the institution you wish to join. As seen on the purpose of most Universities that we have studied they aimed at preparing skilled workers – they did not prepare skilled thinkers, skilled entrepreneurs, or/and skilled job creators but rather those early Universities prepared an ocean of skilled job seekers; essentially Universities graduates especially in Africa were individuals trained to serve and work for others. Universities in Africa served as institution to recruit social elites for the colonial administration and later for political regimes. This mission evolved with independence of African countries[8] – the role of universities became that of producing human capital to meet the needs of the newly independent states. This standpoint is contrary to the American model which at the independence of America the democratic mission was that of training citizens – individuals to self-actualization and in turn serving the society.

The Raison d'être of Universities
Universities in the world – the modern western universities and those following their operation system have evolved over time and so were their raison d'être (mission or purpose of their existence). University raison d'être are dynamic and flexible; they translate education policies, philosophical ideals, and culture of a particular epoch. Since modern western universities started in the 11th century in the medieval period; the major raison d'être of universities kept on changing as they rendered service to different entities such as the church, governments, individuals and the public.

During the medieval period (5th-15th centuries) the church was such an important single institution; all activities evolved around it and so early universities had to serve for the needs and mission of the church. Thus you can see the academics and scholar's thoughts were and /or had to align with the church and its interests (Britanica, n.d; Scott, 2006).

---

[8] Cloete Nico and Maasen Peter 2015

When the world moved to nationalism that is the shift of interest moved to governments that is to nation-states and that leaders became state conscious, universities directed their interests to that side too. Universities became funded by states and thus they had to render their services to governments (Scott.2006)

On the down of liberalism, around 17th and 18th centuries, that is when liberalism took hold of leadership and emphasis put to an individual's freedom, equality, human rights and development – universities became of service to individuals and the state.

The Mission in Nationalization
The service to the government of nation-state in the west modern universities became obvious when universities were nationalized by nation-states. The soundest examples are the monarchies of England, France, and Spain which nationalized their universities funded them and thus they had to serve their nation-state through preparing required personnel for the nation interest[9] (development). The experience today in countries most strong (institutions with reliable funds) are public universities. The United States of America (USA) is an exceptional case as it has not nationalized its universities.

Mission in Democratization
The epoch of democratization in the world was to a large extent, influenced by the USA[10]. The USA became independent on July 4th 1776; that was the independence of 13 American colonies that detached their political links to Great Britain and thus becoming first democratic nation-state in the world (Scott, 2006). In those states, individual rights were highly respected and indeed protected by the nation-state's constitution. The early American leaders were very much influenced by the European Enlightenment which put a grave accent on individual rights and individualism (individual development). The leaders wanted a well educated population as they believed that it was only education that would have ensured the reign of republic values.

---

[9] Scott.2006
[10] Scott.2006 (ibid)

The leaders in newly independent democratic nation-states saw the function of university education in the fulfillment of individual and community needs. The university education had the mission of training an individual to discover his/her talents and abilities that would be used for the betterment of the community (Scott, 2006). This American model of "democrating university education" in my view is the best model and I suggest African universities adopt the model as it trains a person according to their passions and talents and thus preparing job creators through their abilities and talents. In the end individuals get fulfilled and in the due course the society benefits of University graduates.

The Community Outreach Mission

The University role of service to the public of the nation-state arose as a regular mission of USA's Universities through the Morrill Acts of 1862 and 1890[11] the practices from the American Universities were so pragmatic and indeed useful to the society so much that the experience influenced many universities in the world. This model could in a way have been influenced[12] as well by the pragmatic philosophy that was championed by American philosophers such as Charles Sanders Peirce, William James, and John Dewey whose philosophies should have influenced Universities to come up with a curriculum that answers to public problems.

Graduates and Employment in Africa

Conventional wisdom is when a University student completes their studies, they would be engaged in a job putting to practice the skills he has acquired as a student. Engaging graduates is desired for a prosperous economy. The young person from school, in most cases, is full of skills and knowledge and at times completely new knowledge / technology that would improve production or better the offered services. Bearing this fact to mind well organized economies foster

---

[11] The Morrill Acts, among other issues shifted the education curriculum from classical to applied system of education. Solicit funds for colleges in each state and education be accessed by all citizens including African Americans

[12] www.history.state.gov/milestones/1776-1783/declaration

University studies thus many young people join university studies, for universities act as incubators of development of talents and skillful personnel who would in turn, through their work, stir up economic growth which influence economic development.

However, this conventional wisdom does not apply to Africa or to most African countries. The continent has the least number of young people joining tertiary studies where the gross enrollment ratio for university studies is less than 10 percent for most African countries – specifically sub Saharan Africa with the exception of only three to four countries: South Africa, Botswana, Mauritius (Cloete, et al.2015). Having a small number of graduates would mean that they all get absorbed into the employment market- alas that is not the case in the continent. The graduates, despite the small number compared to other regions of the world, fail to secure an employment opportunity when they finish their studies (Going global, 2014). There are a number of reasons leading to that situation; for some countries it is caused by stagnant economic growth failing to create job opportunities, for others it is lack of required skills in the job market. Indeed the causes of graduates' unemployment are complex; other reasons include lack of information about job opportunities, lack of links between university and employers, graduates lacking skills needed in the job market, and stagnant economies failing to create new job opportunities. These reasons of lack of employment to graduates define our problem and indeed the purpose of writing this chapter and thus influencing the book's idea.

Employability of African Graduates
Employability is defined by Going global as the possession of required knowledge, skills and other attributes that enable the obtaining and maintaining of decent employment. In a study by Going global that involved four countries in the continent: Nigeria, South Africa, Ghana and Kenya, – the figure of unemployed graduates and those of the age of graduates, for countries without specific figures of graduates, was right. In Nigeria the percentage of unemployment for graduates stood at 23.1%, South Africa at 5.9%, 41.6% in Ghana and in Kenya it was 15.7%. A survey by the inter-University Council for East Africa

(IUCEA) revealed in 2014 disturbing facts. Their survey argued that between 51 and 63 percent of the graduates were found to be "half-baked" unfit for employment and lacking required job market skills. The worst were recorded in Uganda at 63% and in Tanzania at 61%. In a desktop study in Tanzania that involved 100 human resources officers, it was found out that Tanzanian graduates were of poor quality and/or of average quality and thus lacked required attributes of employability (Mwita, 2018).

Employers and the Ability of Graduates
The Tanzanian case mentioned above is not an isolated one; there are concerns in the whole of sub Saharan Africa. Employers find some good qualities in graduates such as disciplinary knowledge of what they have studied, however, there are some important soft and hard skills that they miss such as IT, personal attributes such as trustworthiness, reliability and pragmatic skills such as team working and ability to solve problems. In a study carried out in Nigeria, among other findings, it revealed a significant "skills discrepancies" between what was required by an employer and what a graduate possessed. The discrepancy was more pronounced in the areas of communication, IT, decision making, and critical thinking (Oketch et al. 2014). The case studies and findings of these kinds are in large number; in this study only a few are cited and these ones should suffice to explain the matter, and thus empower and encourage you and I develop skills that we need and are as well required by employers so as to solve the problems facing you, our youth, the communities around us and our economies.

Universities and Quality of Graduates in Africa

Universities are the power houses expected to empower young people with skills. Universities should offer skills depending on the needs of young people and not much as we witness in many institutions students simply studying what is offered; few students study what is of their interest otherwise they only take what is offered. The acquired knowledge is normally diverse from medicine to engineering, philosophy, sociology, languages, history, commerce, law, architecture, and much more, however the discipline should be accompanied with necessary soft skills such as independent thinking, critical thinking, financial education, decision making and more is needed to help students exploit their talents, passions so that they work well in their future work and carriers and thus live a fulfilled life. To succeed in offering such skills to students, universities have a number of tasks to carry out:

1. *Quality Teaching and Learning*

Universities play a great role in the formation of their graduates. The formation of graduates is supposed to be holistic so that a graduate balances in all spheres; declaring interest I myself am a dualist; I take a human person as a single being, however composed of body and soul. The two parts have their needs which need to be met so as to have a balanced human person. Providing too much to the needs of the body will lead into consumerism syndrome where as providing too much to the soul will lead to fundamentalism, and hence the necessity of a balanced formation of graduates.

Preparing competent graduates holistically requires a number of ingredients/ attributes. Studies revealed that good teaching and learning quality in the degree programs is the major factor facilitating graduates' employability. This factor should be complemented with important skills including soft skills such as trustworthiness, perseverance, honesty, and hard work. Moreover, pragmatic skills such as problem solving skills, decision making skills, written and oral communication skills are as well essential for their success. Currently in many sub Saharan African Universities, there is poor learning environment for students and thus there is need of improving the infrastructure of the universities, enabling staff on on-going training and structures that facilitate students' teaching and learning (Going Global, 2014)

In the past when university studies were a privilege of a few nobilities much learning for the rest of the population was through apprenticeship; one would work with the master in his laboratory, workshop or any other kind of office normally for a number of years at times up to seven years. The apprentice worked hard enough to acquire the desired carrier for his life would depend on the same. After that amount of time one was considered competent in that field (Green, 2012).

2. Multiple Learning Experiences

When university studies were a privilege of a few nobilities much learning was through apprenticeship as mentioned above; one would work with the master in his laboratory, workshop normally for a period of up to seven years. After that amount of time one was considered competent in that field (Green, 2012). A learner would observe carefully what his master was doing; he would learn by doing what the master was doing and he asked the master to assist in some workshop works.

Michael Faraday (1791-1867) serves as a good example of an individual who excelled in the field of electromagnetism through apprenticeship. Though he was brought up in poverty he refused to remain in that situation – he worked hard to discover his talents through extra ordinary love of reading books, in the books he found his passion and interest in science and started following the lectures in science of his future master, Humphry Davy. He went on to learn from and though his master Humphry Davy. He persevered so much by observing what his master was doing, did more than what Davy asked him to do, he got the opportunity as well of being exposed through the work of his master. The climax was when he got the opportunity to work as a laboratory assistant to Davy at the Royal Institution. He worked so hard up to the point when he was able to discover what became his strength and contribution to the world, and the rest in now history (Green, 2012).

A study in South Africa has revealed that field work experience, which is a practical part of what students learn in classrooms, complemented greatly what students learn in classrooms, and it greatly influenced chances for graduates to secure a decent job. Job advertisements in several African countries demand for work experience of several years. This means fresh graduates cannot qualify for the job opportunities. This puzzle of work experience could be solved successfully by graduates themselves and their respective Universities. When they are still at campus students should engage themselves on acquiring the working and learning experience through volunteering in the offices, workshops, firms, industries related with their study discipline. Moreover, they can get involved in some kind of community service which will provide for them the learning and working experience too. Universities need to incorporate field work in all their programs so as to provide another learning platform for students. Universities should encourage students to continue with volunteering and rendering of service in the community. Experience shows that students who carry out seriously the practical part of their studies get to know the community and master the discipline they are acquiring better than those who don't do that and so stand a great chance to secure decent employment opportunities.

3. *The Liaison of Graduates with (to) Employers*
The link of graduates and employers is essential for securing of decent jobs. After the university studies community service and volunteering, it is time for graduates to commit themselves to serious work life. Universities should facilitate the link between graduates and employers. From my experience of a few universities that I have been to in Sub Saharan Africa, I realized that most or all of them do not explicitly have the service of linking students and employers. It is advised that universities establish careers advisory services and job fairs where university students and graduates would meet with employers hear directly from them and get to know of their requirements and demands. It would be a good occasion for employers as well to look for talents of their choices.

At this moment and for the purpose of helping graduates, universities could also establish a unit that is responsible in filling the gaps that are left out by university programs. It should be the moment to address pragmatic skills that are needed in the job market such as problem solving skills, written and oral communication skills, ICT skills and above all entrepreneurship skills. Entrepreneurship skills are of great importance because they empower an individual to think of employing himself/ herself. Entrepreneurship skills are necessary because they make a graduate become creative and could come up with new approaches to work if employed or in personal entrepreneurial activities. And lastly, Universities need to involve employers in their programs preparations so as to accommodate skills and other expertise needed by industries that employ graduates; this partnership would greatly improve production in industries on one hand and competent and employable graduates on the other side[13].

In the study by Oketch et al. (2014) on the impact of tertiary education on development; they found out that: University education influence positively earnings of individual graduates. On macro-economy, there was strong evidence that university education contributed substantially to economic growth. Moreover, the study identified evidence of positive impact brought about by graduates at workplaces.

Furthermore, the impact of University education was revealed on the capability of graduates in strengthening institutions. Their impact was more revealed in sectors of health, gender equality, nutrition, democratization. The study has clearly identified that earnings of individual graduate was more pronounced and evident than in any other sectors. Thus findings from this study show that despite weaknesses in our universities their contribution in well recognized though in a limited share. Now what should be done to improve our universities what nature and type of universities do we need.

Following the analyses of university literature, experience from graduates university students across some universities, I find that the American model of universities, as presented in the literature reviewed, is the best model as it looks and invests on an individual's self-fulfillment. When an individual is self-fulfilled through education then their give back to community becomes even greater. If you are a graduate and wish to contribute more significantly to the economy of

---

[13] This kind of partnership is very much being emphasized by the Tanzania Commission for Universities. That a University should consult all necessary stakeholders before and during preparations of a program so as to ensure its relevance to the community

your country, and wish to live a fulfilled life, then you have to know yourself better than before, get to know your passion and talents so that when selecting a university program you choose one that aligns well with your talents.

Further Readings

Cloete Nico and Maasen Peter. 2015. Roles of Universities and the
        African context
Cloete, Nico, Maassen Peter and Pillay Pundy.2015. Higher Education
        and National Development. International Encyclopedia:
        meanings and purposes of Higher Education
De Ridder – Symoens (ed).2003. A History of the University in
        Europe, volume I Universities in the Middle Ages Cambridge
        University Press, Cambridge
Going Global. 2014. Can Higher education solve Africa's
        job crisis? Understanding graduate employability in
        sub Saharan Africa. British Council
Green, Robert. 2012. Mastery, Penguin Group. New York
Mwita, Kelvin. 2018. Tanzania Employability: Perception of
        Human Resource Management Practitioners
Oketch Moses, McCowan Tristan, and Schendel Rebecca.2014. The
        impact of Tertiary Education on Development. A rigorous
        Literature Review. Department of International Development.
        UK
Pelikan, Jaraslav.1992. The Idea of a the University: A Reexamination.
        Yale University. New Haven
Scott. C. John 2006. The Mission of the Universities: Medieval to Post
        Modern Transformations. The journal of Higher Education,
        vol.77.no.1

CHAPTER TWO

Self-Awareness

Self-awareness is the act of being conscious of one self as to what you are, who you are, what your capabilities are, what your limitations are, how you can be able to overcome your limitations and use your strengths to succeed and prosper in life through your talents which enable you create your life purpose and thus live a fulfilled life.

Who are You?

This is an important question that everybody needs to ask oneself in life. When did you last ask yourself this question, if you have ever attempted it at all?

Many of us from a certain age become aware of oneself at the conscious level that allows us to know that we are male or female; we know our biological background; many of us up to the level of grandparents; some of us even met them before they passed away; we know where originally we come from, and much more about our biological families. However, do you know what you can do and/or what you should be doing? As part of self-awareness and knowledge of one self, some of us through studies are aware of how our bodies operate from the biological plane.

You many know that the human body is a complex reality composed of cells, tissues, organs, systems, and so on. Those individual parts of the body operate together without our conscious and/or without our efforts; it is automatic and very much efficient.

The human body, as you are aware of it, has five organs which are vital for the survival and wellbeing of a human person. The proper survival and functioning of the human person depends on the five organs namely; the brain, heart, liver, kidneys and lungs. The brain coordinates all other organs as it sends and receives signals from the other four organs through specialized means of communication done through secreted hormones and the nervous system.

The vital organs are connected together through biological systems – the body systems carry out specific daily functions for everyday living. The body systems include the circulatory, digestive, endocrine, immune, lymphatic, nervous, muscular, reproductive, skeletal, respiratory, and urinary.

Functions of Individual Systems
The circulatory system transports blood, nutrients, oxygen, carbon dioxide, and hormones around the human body. The digestive system, in cooperation with several organs breaks down and absorbs food nutrients and removes wastes from the body. The endocrine system secretes hormones into the blood which regulates various functions in the body against bacteria, viruses and other enemies of the body. The nervous system controls both voluntary and involuntary actions and sends signals to different parts of the body. The reproductive system is engaged on human reproduction; this is the system that ensures continuity of the human race. The muscular system is involved in bodily movement, blood flow and other functions in the body. The lymphatic system is involved in producing and letting the lymph circulate in the body to help protect the body against bodily enemies. The respiratory system enables you take in clear air known as oxygen and expel dirty air known as carbon dioxide; this is the process we call breathing. The urinary system excretes waste materials from the body particularly a waste product known as urea[14].

The systems and organs in the body cooperate and function harmoniously to enable proper functioning of your body. Though the human body is more complex, the vital organs and the systems should suffice to show you that you, as a human person, are such a complex being; capable of doing great things in the world. Most of the activities

---

[14] www.livescienne.com

in the human body carry on their functions without your awareness, consciousness or any contribution from you; the body simply does what it is meant to be doing without consulting you. Thus, the moment you become aware of your life and how extraordinary you are, as a human being, then, great wonders may occur in your life when you decide to do so. This is because there is so much greatness in you than you may imagine.

The complexity of a human body that we have just observed paints a picture of your capability. Through your brain you are capable of doing so much than you have ever brought it to consciousness. To see what you can be or can accomplish look at what other human beings, of the same make up as you, have done. When you reflect and scrutinize the reason behind successful people who have gone down in history you realize that they were pushed by dedication, hard work, sense of purpose, and perseverance in what they were doing.

Successful people almost all of them are those who realized what they had as hidden gifts in them, they became conscious of the passions and talents in them and worked hard in many hours, days, weeks, months, and years to realize their true call, true mission in life. Everybody including you has a task a mission that you need to fulfill in life before you finish your life here on Earth. When you are able to do what is in you that is when you become a successful person. Success, according to Munrose Myles, is to discover your mission in life that is embedded in you and be able to accomplish it before you die. When you are able to do what is in you that is when you become a successful person. A successful person in most cases comes up with a product, an invention, a discovery, a solution that addresses some problems in life or that helps improve the living standards of a human person. Entrepreneurs say a person who through his/her invention solves community problems not only does s/he become successful but also attracts wealth to him/herself. In other words most wealth individuals have been able to solve certain society's problems – that is what you too are capable of doing. However, one cannot realize any greatness in them unless they know who they are. Do you know who are you? What are you studying? Why are you studying the program that you are pursuing? Did you take time to reflect on who you are, what you are capable of doing? Did you take time to read and investigate on the mission of a University that you are studying at? Is it in line with your abilities, passion and talents? What will you do when you finish your studies?

Science through biology tells us that the biological awareness is useful and informative because it informs us that we are what we are because of the inherited biological traits through the genes coming from both of our parents. This fact to a large extent defines every one of us. Some of the inherited aspects include; talents, behavior, all that portrays us as individuals giving us our height, skin colour, colour of our eyes and much more.

The inherited gifts in you remain hidden in you up to when you develop them. The talents, behavior all of them are in you as good seeds. They need favorable condition for them to grow and become what they are meant to be; up to when you activate and develop them, they remain dormant buried in you. Discovering them is supposed to be a dedicated and intentional undertaking – you have to decide to cultivate and discover them for you to be able to benefit out of them. However, having a human brain makes you a special being; you are not prisoned to follow some prepared programs; you can become whatever you want, you are capable of creating your life purpose as influenced by your passions and talents.

And so, Who are You?
As we said before knowing who you are will greatly influence what you create as your life purpose and to that effect the success you register in life. When did you last ask yourself that question; who are you? What was the response? Do you live by that response? In most cases, many of us do not have enough time to ask ourselves that question – we are either busy with the job schedule or searching for a job to satisfy our needs our family's and in Africa the extended family is also a large responsibility that one is involved with. As for you a University student, you could be busy with school projects, class assignments, and other related school activities. Such activities define you as a university student. Despite your busy university program the question is still

pertinent to you too. Do you take time to know yourself? A strange question isn't? Does knowing yourself a strange question?

Many of us know ourselves only at the surface level; that is you know your parents, your grandparents, your clan, knowing where you come from. However, we do not know at the depth level of who we are. What about you, do you know yourself at the depth level? It is possible as well that you do not know why you find yourself at the University where you are studying. You passed your examinations, got yourself selected by the institution where you are because your friends influenced you. There is nothing wrong being advised especially by your friends the people you trust. The problem is; you have not been active about your institution; you have not bothered to inquire or/and know the vision and mission (the raison d'être) of your university where you are a student. It is indeed difficult for you to bother about the raison d'être of your university if you have never bothered to find out your raison d'être of your life. Who are you, what are you capable of, what are your talents? What are you supposed to be doing here on Earth? What have planned to do in life?

The university degree that you are studying if you took time to think about and made an informed decision to study it, and if it is in line with your talents and aligns with your purpose in life, then, you can be sure of becoming fulfilled and indeed successful in life.

Take the case of Ben Carson; a fulfilled medical doctor and author of *Gifted Hands* and *The Big Picture* as an example. Ben says that he through different experiences realized that he had a gift of coordination between the brain and his hands. He took time to contemplate, to think about his life and get to know what is the purpose of his being on Earth – he tells us that realization of his talent helped him know what University program to study and thus helping him choose a career in life – creating a purpose of life that is in line with his talents.

Ben Carson is one among few successful individuals that were able to attain fulfillment in life thanks for being able to identify a career that is in line with their talents and created a life purpose that is aligned with his talents. It is a pity that many of us do not know ourselves; and this fact is a weakness which has its own negative consequences. This weakness prevents you from creating your life purpose and become successful in life.

What is Success?
Success is defined differently by different people of diverse background. I prefer the definition and explanation by Dr. Munroe Myles, a fulfilled motivational speaker and author of a number of bestselling books that have been of great help to many in the society. He argues that success is the completion and effective fulfillment of the original purpose for your existence. Success comes through self-awareness that enables you discover your gifts, talents and thus create your life purpose and complete it before you die. Success is not measured by what you do compared by what others do.

Socrates urged his disciples to journey into self-discovery in his famous saying: "*man know thyself.*" Knowing oneself enables one to know their strengths and weaknesses. This is useful as it helps one know how to live well with others in life and be successful.

There are various tools that are designed to help you know yourself; one of them is the JOHARI Window. The window was invented by two Psychologists Joseph Luft and Harry Ingham; taking the initial of their first names Joseph and Harry. The window helps individuals in self-awareness as it helps us understand ourselves. The two psychologists developed the tool because they believed that whatever happens in your life depends on your own self-awareness, the choices you make and the life purpose you create for yourself.

Table 1: The JOHARI Window

Open Window	Blind Window
Hidden Self	Unknown Self

Open Window

The open window is an area of self-awareness where what is in that area is known by you and all those around you. It includes the information, behavior, characteristics that you know them and all your friends know them.

Blind Window

This window contains the information, behavior and characteristics about you that are known to all others around you except to you only. This is equivalent to a dark/blind spot that you need to open it and get the resources found in it. You can get the richness of this area by asking for feedback from your entourage and by being open to feedback from friends and those around you in general. If you work honestly on the feedback from those close to you then the area of the blind window reduces and that enables you to know yourself better.

Hidden Window

In this space you have the information that is only known to you. This could be useful information to you and the community around you and even mankind in general and thus keeping it hidden is a waste of your gifts and indeed very much selfishness. Through self-awareness you realize your talents, and purpose of your life on Earth, consequently you will open up this window so as to harness the gifts and thus become a successful person in life.

Unknown Window

In the unknown window there is information that is not known to you and those surrounding you. You can be able to discover your talents, gifts, abilities through self-development: reading books on self-development, opening up yourself to your friends and experiences.

The Johari Window is a good tool to helping you know yourself. Once you know yourself then everything you do in life should be in line to what you are. The knowledge of oneself helps us to discovering our talents and gifts which help you create your life purpose. We have learnt that one becomes successful in life only when they fulfill their purposes in life. For a University student and for a prospective one; this discovery should guide you to choose a University that offers a program that is in line with your life purpose.

How to Select a University Program

For you a university student did you take time to reflect, scrutinize and digest the vision and mission of the University where you are at the moment as a student? Did you take time to reflect, carry out an investigation on the purpose of the program that you are pursuing?

These questions and more of the same line of thought are vital for your success in life. I am bringing up these questions out of my personal experience and of a score of colleagues; former class mates at secondary school, university and even at work did not take enough time to ponder on those questions. So long as they passed their examinations, just like in a factory conveyor belt, most of us (they) were pushed to the next level unprepared or un informed about the programs we pursued.

Some of us selected university programs following the influence of our friends; others joined programs because of the market influence and different adverts. There is nothing wrong for us being attracted to the programs through adverts; the matter is; we should have taken time to ponder about the programs. We should have asked ourselves what is the purpose of the program; what can it help a student acquire in terms of knowledge, skills and competences.

You need to think and reflect on the programs' expected learning outcomes (ELOs), the university's vision and mission; compare it with your purpose in life. Before you select a university to study at, before you select a program to pursue at the tertiary level of education, you need to find out or create your purpose in life. Why are you on Earth? What is the purpose of you being born, what are you born for? What are you going to contribute to the world? Which University, which program(s) do you think can be able to fulfill you as an individual? or at least equip you with the tools you need in life? Select a program that has ELOs that relate to your talents and which promises to arm you with the knowledge, skills and competences that you are going to need in your career to fulfill the purpose of you being here on Earth. To use the words of Gabriel Marcel – you and everybody else are travellers; travelling towards your destination in life. The task ahead of you is which university and program could act as a means of transport to see you at your destination safely and successfully?

If you select a university and program while bearing in mind your strength, talents, dreams and aptitudes then you are likely to gain the right knowledge, the required skills in your future career and the competence needed for you to live the purpose of your life here on Earth. When you select a program while adhering to all those requirements in mind then you are likely to create your own business or secure an activity immediately after completion of your university study, that is possible even if the University as we saw in chapter one prepares mainly people who are going to be working (personnel, human resources) for others. My take is Universities should prepare individuals to become what they are meant to be or what they want to create in life- the individuals should be creative and pragmatic thinkers!

Selection of your university and program should, as already mentioned, be guided and informed by your passions, talents, strength, capabilities and dreams that you possess in your life. Knowing your passions, talents and capabilities require your dedication to knowing yourself. You need to learn how to know yourself; how to know yourself is crucial and indeed necessary for success in life.

How Do you Know Yourself?

Knowing oneself is vital for a successful life on Earth. We have seen already that you become successful only when you do what you were created to do on Earth or what you have created as your life purpose. The problem that hinders many of us from living a successful life is that we do not know how to arrive to the purpose of our life.

There are many distractions that bury deep down the purpose of our life. Our modern life is full of noise, adverts, *"junky life style just as you have junky food."* We do not take time to reflect on our lives sufficiently. I call upon you on taking time to retrospect and reflect on your life; depending on your temperament, it could take some few minutes or hours all dedicating that time to see how you live your daily life. You can make it a habit. You may decide to make it even more systematic and so have a monthly recollection. The practice of monthly recollection; I have it thanks to my experience in a religious life that I experimented for some years.

For your monthly recollection, you can do it the way you prefer. The monthly recollection based on my personal experience is that; you go somewhere away from your working environment; you go to a place that will disconnect you from your habitual daily activities; a noiseless place is more desirable. In your monthly recollection, basically, you will be taking stock of your monthly activities. You are in charge of your life, depending on your purpose of life; you decide whether it is a spiritual stock taking, business stock taking, entrepreneurial stock taking, and innovative business stock taking and so on. You have to do this exercise in an honest way – it is your life that you are dealing with and that truthfulness to yourself is of paramount importance. The intention of the recollection is to correct/repair where things did not go as planned and forecast how the future should behave. You may decide to lead your own recollection all by yourself or you may have someone guiding you on how to do it.

My Personal Experience on Talents

Discovering one's passions and talents is not an easy thing to everybody, however it is a possible reality; it has been done by many individuals, it is being done today by a multitude of individuals, and you too can do it now. There is no a one formula fits all for everybody to discover their passions and talents there could be as many approaches as there are people out there. However, the good thing is that you can learn from what others have done to discover your passions and talents if you have not discovered them yet. Here is part of what helped me discover my passions and talents that lead me to creation of my life purpose.

When I was a primary school pupil, I developed a reading habit, and I guess the habit was triggered by my father. I remember one evening my father narrated to us (my sisters, brothers and I) a story from the Bible. I do not remember if he was reading from the Bible or simply narrating it from his head. He told us the story of Moses from the book of Exodus. It was about Moses and the burning stick that did not get burn out. Exodus 3: 1-22; 4: 1-17. That story and incident fascinated and marked me so much that I started reading books. I acquired membership in a local library where I would borrow different books and read them at home. I also bought some books from my personal money. It happened that even at primary school, I had some personal money as on weekends and during holidays; I worked on construction sites as an assistant fellow sending bricks, sand and activities of the kind to the *fundis*. I also carried out some small business such as selling roasted groundnuts, oranges, pieces of sugar cane around town. This small business kept on expanding to a good level, unfortunately I did not continue with the business as I had to concentrate in studies rather than business.

Following that developed habit of reading books, I one time bought a book that changed my life forever. The book was titled "**Don Bosco Rafiki wa Vijana**" I read from page one up to the last. I was fascinated by the life of John Bosco; a young person from Turin. I was even more moved by the way he so much cared for the young persons; I was impressed by his efforts of establishing an association that cared for the youth. That spirit of John Bosco; caring for youth through different activities continue even today through a society he founded called Salesians of Don Bosco. When I finished reading *Don Bosco Rafiki wa*

Vijana, I found the contact and physical address of the school that prepare young persons who would later join the association and take care of youth in the streets. I wrote to them explaining my interest to joining them in their undertaking. I was invited to attend a *come and see workshop* where at the end of it all, I was selected to join them for studies and training, and the rest is now part of history.

Another behavior that has helped me discover my talents is the interest of letter writing that my brothers and I developed. As we grew up at home, we had access to a postal box; our father paid for an annual subscription fee. I do not remember exactly how or what prompted the interest of letter writing amongst us. What I know and remember now is that my brothers and I developed a habit of writing to different organizations in the world such as radio stations, business firms where by, in response, they would send us various items such as photos, gifts such as Walkman, magazines, newsletters, post cards, calendars etc. such items developed in me the reading and writing habits as I was exposed to those items of different art and literature.

Furthermore, the college where I studied *The Philosophy Center of Jinja* (PCJ) and the residential formation house where I lived *Lavigerie House* had both college and house journals respectively. Contribution of the articles in both journals came mainly from students themselves. I was a seasonal contributor to both journals as I sent in several articles for publication. In one of the issues a lecturer read one of my articles and told me that it was a good piece as it was so much educative. The comments from my lecturer were so much strong that they had a big impact in my life. Since then, I have continued to write articles and books on different themes because my lecturer assured me that the articles I once wrote had content that would be useful to some individuals' lives. Thus paying attention to what others say about you, your products is extremely important for it can give us very substantial information that reveals who real you are and what your passions and talents could be.

Dear reader, you too can follow a similar approach to discovering your strength and talents by reflecting on your early life. It is through such a life that you recognize some power sleeping in you. You just need to awake and put it to the service of others and yours too. This exercise of travelling back to your early life to search for your capabilities and talents is real and effective. Everybody on Earth has talents that demonstrate themselves at a certain point in life. When you pay enough attention to your early life you will definitely get the answer or at least some clues of what your talents are. If for some reasons you are not able to recall such memories then consult your elders; your older siblings, parents, relatives or even your parents' neighbors as you grew and teachers where you studied while you were still a minor.

The Path to Talents

Researchers argue that we have passions and talents that could guide us on how to create our life purpose. Thierry Dubois in his book *le livre pour découvrir vos talents* written after years of experience gives us precise path and exercises to discover our talents. Howard Gardner, a scholar at Harvard University in his book *Frame of Mind: The Theory of Multiple Intelligences* suggests that all human beings have at least eight intelligences. Where do you find yourself in, which of these suggested paths speak more about you find out yourself:

1. *Linguistic*: this path involves individuals that have talents in the field of linguistic. Are you attracted to word games, poems, jokes, and tongue twisters? Do you use words convincingly and correctly? If you feel attracted to this area, then language which includes reading, writing, and speaking could be your natural talents. You could be able to write clearly, instruct and or communicate through talks.

2. *Logical*: This path concerns individuals who operate activities involved with this field. Do you like ordered things, facts, data, and use numbers efficiently? If you feel attracted to this area then numbers, logic, critical thinking, reasoning and mathematical problem answering then logic could be your natural talent. You feel things operate best by taking a rational, ordered and logical path to life.

3. *Spatial:* This path concerns mostly those with imagination and perceive the world in colours and shapes accurately. If you are attracted to this area then thinking in pictures and images using shapes and colours to foresee the world around you then most probably this is your talent. You can visualize, paint, draw and sketch your ideas in images.

4. *Musical :* Do you like making vibrating tunes, or singing along with the TV and radio? Do you enjoy and understand rhythm? If you are attracted to this path, then rhythms and melodies; singing in time and having an ear for music are your natural talents. Work on this and develop your talent.

5. *Kinesthetic:* This concerns those who are interested in exercise, playing sports, and working with their hands. Do you move your body efficiently? If you feel attracted to this path then handling objects, demonstrating athletic prowess are your natural ability. You are capable of putting things together, dance and enjoy physical activities of all kinds.

6. *Interpersonal:* Do you like to put on the shoes and feelings of others? Do you easily relate with others including in the teamwork? If you are attracted to this area, then looking into the needs, feelings and desires of others, understanding and working with others are your natural talents. You are capable of observing the world from others' perception and connect effectively with the people around you.

7. *Intrapersonal;* Do you like to meditate or reflect on the imponderables / mysteries? Are you enticed to solitude and reflection? If you are attracted to this area, then being self-directed, aware of the inner self and inner feelings are your natural talents. You are able to spend time alone to reflect on the world around you independently, self-disciplined and in self-motivated way.

8. *Naturalistic;* Do you like to analyze how things fit together? If you are attracted to this area, then sensing, understanding and systematically ordering the natural world are your natural abilities. You have an intuitive sense of how things fit together and are able to distinguish interrelationships in the world (Leider, 2004).

What if the Exercise Takes Long?

People who succeed in life have a combination of factors accompanying them. One of those factors of success is perseverance. Perseverance is the ability to continue with your undertaking even when things seem to be hard. Perseverance proofs to be of great importance even to individuals so much talented in a certain field. Talent is defined as the natural ability to perform some activities easily, efficiently and naturally without employing much energy. An individual talented in a sport, say football, such as Mbwana Samatta, Victor Wanyama, Kalusha Bwalya, Austin Okocha, these footballers though they are (were) talented but they still need the success factors of professional discipline and perseverance. They have to keep on exercising themselves, training, follow the instructions of their coach, bear in mind the dos and don'ts of a successful footballer. Keeping in mind and practicing the regulations is an indicator of a successful person, and that is perseverance.

Perseverance works best when one has discovered/ decided on what they are going to do in life. What should you as a student who wants to be something but are not sure what you exactly want to accomplish in life? If you find yourself in such a situation whereby despite much effort in order to help you discover your passions and talents and deciding on what you want to do in life in the name of your life purpose, but you can't still discover your passions, then the following chapters are essential to you as a successful individual in life.

If you are a university student who has not yet been able to discover your passions and talents and that would help you decide on what your life purpose should be, as it is the case for many students who have not discovered their passions and talents, then the following skills are useful for you, other students and anybody else in life. I call upon you to develop these skills which I assure you could be very useful and indeed pragmatic in life. This call is substantiated by Angus & Larson, 2011; that skills for identifying goals, decision making and others are becoming extremely important in the labour market and in self-employment.

> Independent Thinking
> Logical Thinking
> Critical Logical
> Strategic Thinking
> Creative Thinking
> Positive Thinking
> Thinking in systems

These skills will help you in discovering your passions and talents that would help you create or decide on what should be THE PURPOSE OF YOUR LIFE and thus help you live a pragmatic, happy, successful, and fulfilled life while contributing to society.

Further Readings

Angus, M. Rachel & Larson, W. Reed. 2011. Adolescents'
        Development of Skills for Agency in youth Programs: Learning
        to Think Strategically. Child Development, January/ February,
        Volume 82, Number 1, Page 277-294
Dubois, Thierry. 2015. Le Livre Pour Découvrir Vos Talents.
        Eyrolles. Paris
Ukleja, Mick and Lorber, L. Robert. 2009. Who are you what
        do you want? Penguine Group, New York
Gardner, Howard. 1985. Frame of Mind: The Theory of
        Multiple Intelligences: The Basic Book. New York

Green, Robert. 2012. Mastery, Penguin Group. New York

Leider J. Richard. 2004. The Power of Purpose.
        Berrett-Koehler Publishers, Inc. San Francisco

CHAPTER THREE

Thinking Independently

Independent thinking involves two realities that we need to clarify before we proceed to the main business. Defining the two terms gives us the authority to move on unambiguously and thus get the right information, we are looking for, on the subject matter of independent thinking.

The term "Independent" is an adjective from the noun "independence". The later means a state of being free from another authority, self-rule, liberty, freedom. It is a state where one is in control of the situation.

Thinking is one of the mental activities; it is one of many activities of the brain which coordinates activities of all organs and systems in your body. Thus, thinking is an action or means of using your mind to produce thoughts.

Therefore, independent thinking occurs when an individual produces his/her own original thoughts after doing their mental assignment in the mind[15]. It is the ability of an individual to be able to think on their own and present their thoughts before others. Independent thinking is the capacity to employ rationality, neutral and objective view on all issues concerning spheres of life: social problems, organizational affairs, team work affairs and individual problems. It includes the ability to use

---

[15] It is necessary to differentiate the mind from the brain. The brain is one among the physical, tangible organs of your body whereas the mind is invisible; it is part of the metaphysical world of ideas, feeling, thinking, imagination – the brain is mostly associated with the mind and consciousness, however, the mind is not tied only to the brain – the intelligence of the mind (*being able to read from within*) has great influence over all activities of the body: cells, organs, systems all

multiple perspectives to analyse and interpret certain phenomenon (Chen, 2008). Thus, independent thinking is a necessary skill for an individual to stand on his/her own and contribute confidently original thoughts to the world.

Why Independent Thinking?
The source of innovation, inventions and advancement of technology

Independent thinking is necessary and crucial for those aspiring to prosper, contribute to community and in a developed and open minded society. It is the source of innovation, inventions, discoveries and other kind of development. Its importance to you as a university student cannot be over emphasized. It is vital for a true learned person; a true learned person is one who is capable of producing their individual, sensible, meaningful and original thoughts. As a university student you are expected by the society to be able to explain issues in your own understanding way which essentially is a product of independent thinking. University students are expected to be independent thinkers because as according to Julius Nyerere, an African independent thinker himself, a university in the world has the task of training a human person on how to think independently and acquire skills enabling him become capable and responsible in solving community problems (Mandalu, 2019).

University, in the formal education system, is the highest level of education an individual can attain. If it is the highest possible level of education then a university student is expected to come up with exceptional knowledge, skills and competence that those who have not reached that stage cannot easily possess or be easily compared to him. Moreover, the tools, techniques that one acquires at University should be able to address, solve his/her community problems. One of the tools you as a university student needs to possess is independent thinking. As an independent thinker you are expected to use scientific criteria and universal value systems to examine issues at stake. As a university student, scholar and independent thinker you should be able to employ new approaches and be different from other members in the gathering (Chen, 2008).

Independent thinking is vital because it has so much benefit to you as an individual and to the society; some include but not limited to the following:

- It opens to you a great potential of hidden wealth of knowledge
- It empowers you to become a discerning person on what you hear, see even on what your community believes on/in.
- It helps you purify what are regarded as values while in the real sense they are not.
- Independent thinking helps you in increasing performance, productivity, efficiency and thus attain the highest level of self-awareness which as we saw in chapter two leads you to the discovery of an ocean of your gifts and talents leading you to a purposive, happy, and fulfilled life.

Moreover, independent thinking helps you in making informed decisions in your studies, community activities and even in your profession. In fact, if you wish to become successful in your career, you need to have the ability of making sound decisions. You can arrive to informed decisions only if you are making use of independence in thinking; an independent thinker possesses original thoughts that direct him/her in making informed decisions.

While independent thinking is useful in thousand circumstances; the following two are real important and useful for a young person like you aspiring to be successful in your profession as you bring impact to the community.

Independent Thinking Leading to Self-Employment
We said a successful person discovers their passions and talents which in turn assist them in creating a true life purpose, live it correctly before they die; a successful graduate should be able to discover their talents before they join a university program, so that they study what aligns with the their passions and talents, or by the time they complete their university studies. The discovery of their passions and talents can enable them go for self-employment which could be any legal entrepreneurial activity, or a business that calls you to take risks and

make important informed decisions. It is possible to make informed decisions only if you are capable of producing your own original thoughts. As an entrepreneur you need to have positive attitude and willingness to make independent decisions to be successful in your self-employment undertaking. A self-employed person, in most cases, lives his/her created life purpose.

Team Leader

Leaders have the task of paving a way for others to follow. They have the task of coaching team members on how to progress and in carrying out different tasks for team operations. As a leader you are responsible in answering questions of the team members and give them insight of what is required so as to forge ahead. If as a leader you cannot make good and quick decisions then you will distort your reputation. As a successful and influential leader you have to be able to lead others by using innovative ideas, inventive thoughts, led by example, motivate the team members to explore and achieve the full potential in them for the betterment of individuals and the team. All these activities could be realized through original thinking which surely calls for independence in thinking and the good thing is the capability of you becoming an independent thinker is in you.

How Can you Become an Independent Thinker?

The seeds of everything are in everything else – Anaxagoras

Independent thinking as we have already seen is vital for a successful individual life and to the community where an independent thinker lives in. I personally witnessed, learnt and lived the strength and importance of independent thinking in a religious community life. Members in the religious community as the name suggests were emphasized and encouraged on living a community life; sharing a number of substantial aspects in life mainly; prayers, meals, meetings, and monthly recollections. However the community regulations encouraged individual and personalized prayers, meditation, thinking, and interpretation of issues, individual prayers and then meditation was shared at the community level. I can witness that the meditations and sharing at the community level were very insightful, encouraging, rich and fruitful as they came from individuals who had had time to ponder, meditate, and think on their own. Thus if you wish to become a resourceful and successful independent thinker and benefit your community then the following path is necessary.

1. Examination of Conscious

You need to examine your mind set; you need have interests in understanding how you work, how your thoughts flow, you have to know what inspires and motivates you from shifting negative aspects of living into positive thoughts and action. An independent thinker is normally excited by developing new ideas and positive thinking; thus as you wish to become one then your thoughts have to be focused, logical, analytical[16] and creative. You need have an interest in learning as that spirit attracts more opportunities to develop new ideas and action plan on how to make your thoughts more pragmatic[17].

2. Don't go with the Flow

As we human beings socialize and relate with others and so can we easily get carried away by the discussion and thoughts of others. You have to be conscious, active and realize that what everyone is thinking and doing may not necessarily be the best possible approach or solution to a certain problem. Do not get carried away by other people's approaches to life; think rationally. Consider by your own thoughts and experience from elsewhere what could be the best possible alternative in solving your problem or one in the community; examine its advantages and disadvantages before you pick it as the best possible solution[18]

3. Manage Peer Pressure

In life skills peer pressure is one of the subject matters that we deal with. It is necessary to deal with it because peers are the people close and deer to us such as friends and age mates in our vicinity. Even

---

[16] Analytical is from analysis–the ability and /or process of separating parts from a whole and examining each one of them as to how they function individually and connecting in making a whole function as one unit

[17] www.leadershipexpert.co.uk/ how-become-original-thinker.html

[18] https://content.wisestep.com/develop-independent -thinking/

though these people are closest to us it is not necessary that they have the best ideas and deeds or simply of exemplary to our life. As you wish to become an original thinker take time to analyze logically and critically the doing and thoughts of your peers, do not get pressurized just because all your peers are doing it, after all they could all of them be wrong.

4. Aim to do the Best

When you do your homework and assignments with the purpose of impressing your lecturers you are likely to finish your studies with high flying colours but incompetent. The same thing could be with those who are employed; if their objective is to impress their superiors and for that reason they are ready to take wrong decisions so long as it makes happy their supervisor (bosses) then it follows, even if not necessarily that, these fellows will not be of great use to society. As a student you should always strive to be objective search and research to find out the right responses to the task given – do not simply do or present what your lecturers want to see or hear from you- on the contrary present the best objective matter logically and that will improve your ability to strengthening your self-esteem which in turn will strengthen you as an independent thinker.

5. Employ Logic throughout

We human beings are social animals so announced Aristotle hundreds of years ago and being so we do influence each other in our conducts and doings. As university student you can easily get carried away by the thinking of your peers and friends. For university students it is indeed easy for you to be carried away by the thinking of your friends because it is at this time that you are also searching for a life partner, you wish to be accepted by your peers and so you are likely to follow what they decide. To avoid such unconscious discipleship employ logic[19]. When you think systematically your mind capacity keeps on expanding to making you an original and indeed independent thinker. Do not agree

---

[19] Logic is an inborn tool to everyone which helps us think systematically but very few individuals use it.

to fall into the trap of doing what others are doing even if it is not logical – employ logic throughout in your dealings.

6.   Be Courageous and Ready to Accept Failure

As you develop your skills to become and independent thinker you can be sure that you will come across failure. Be ready and courageous to face failure with and open mind as that will enable you look for new strategies and approaches to reach your goal. As a scholar and future professional in a field of your choice, you need to change your methodologies and approaches but stay focused in your objective, be patient as good results cannot come over night. When you have done all your assignment correctly then be patient to wait for the right moment to come.

Following these steps diligently when you encounter such or similar circumstances will help you sharpen your thinking horizon. At the end of the experience you will indeed be able to develop your ability as an independent thinker; ready to take the many opportunities in the world while focusing on what is truly yours according to your talents and purpose of life. This skill enables you as an individual to carry out your activities in a more serious and in-depth manner; as a scientist it is at this level that you could come up with a discovery, a new theory, or an innovation on how to do something in a completely different way in life; as an artist too you may come up with a novel way of approaching or operating things. As you benefit of the acquired skills you will at the same time be benefiting your society.

At this juncture, it is necessary to put forth this precaution. As you become an independent thinker, you have to be careful not to enter into conflict with other members in the society. As you think independently and more especially when you want to stick to objectivity, you will at times come in conflict with your superiors as your thinking could be opposing their thinking. Thus, in such situations, be prudent on how you present your thoughts; be logical, objective, transparent but use a very respective language that even though you present very concrete issues no body feels offended by the way you do it; be a good communicator.

Further Readings

Chen, Xiao –Ping. 2008. Independent Thinking: A path to
        Outstanding Schorlarship. Management and Organization
        Review 4:3 337-348, University of Washington

www.leadershipexpert.co.uk/ how-become-original-thinker.html

https://content.wisestep.com/develop-independent -thinking/

Green, Robert. 2012. Mastery, Penguin Group. New York

CHAPTER FOUR

Thinking Logically

Logic is regarded as a science, an art and or a skill enabling us to think effectively, analyse, argue and communicate systematically, clearly and make sense. It is a skill that informs all other disciplines and our daily life. Logic is a necessary skill but not taught in many countries including in the American education system (McInerny, 2004).

Lack of logical skills in the USA is observed through some bright people who do not portray brilliance when it comes to being logical. They have the capability to thinking logically, that is, clearly and effectively, but fail to demonstrate it in their presentations; the possible and likely explanation is; they have not developed the skill properly, indicating weaknesses in their education system (McInerny, 2004). The American experience is not an isolated case; it is also witnessed in Africa and elsewhere. In East Africa, I have seen students with very high scores in their certificates, but fail to demonstrate their ability at work. Such weaknesses point out deficiency in our education systems. The students' flying colours results demonstrate mastery of subject matter in class. However, they fail to demonstrate it in real life; they lack the skills of transforming class knowledge to real life experience such as connecting education skills with job skills. That is, a logical transfer of skills. Thus, thinking logically and presenting your ideas in the logical manner is indeed essential for you to be accepted in the society as a valuable, active, and contributive person for one to be able to be a logical person. There should be a match between what is in your ideas and objects in the real world. In order for you to be able to become a logical person, there are ten (10) important attitudes that you need to observe:

1. Being attentive,
2. Getting the facts straight,
3. Origin of ideas,
4. Be mindful of the origins of ideas
5. Relate ideas to facts
6. Relate words to ideas
7. Effective communication
8. Be careful with vague and ambiguous language
9. Avoid evasive language (being indirect)
10. Truth

1. Being Attentive

As a university student and an effective member in the society wishing to be logical, you need to be keen when reasoning. Mistakes in reasoning are committed because we don't pay enough attention especially in the familiar situations we find ourselves in. The familiarity of the situation causes us to make careless judgment and decisions. Many times, we suppose that a familiar situation will be a repetition of what we have experienced before. We forget the fact that "you cannot step twice in the same river." That is, every situation is unique and thus you must pay attention to its uniqueness. Attentiveness requires you to be active to individuals, places and things that constitute the situation. You are called to look and see, hear and listen. Train your mind to focus on details including small things for they lead to big ones (McInerny, 2004)

2. Getting the Facts Straight

The Cambridge dictionary defines fact as something that is known to have happened or to exist that for which proof exists or about which there is information. There are two basic types of objective facts, things and events.

A thing is a really existing entity, house, animal, plant etc. Muhimbili hospital is a fact of the first category – it is a thing. Death of Julius

Nyerere is a fact of the second category – it is an event. The fact of event depends on the first fact to some extent – an event occurs at a given place. Julius Nyerere died at St. Thomas hospital, in London; actually you can visit the hospital and observe it directly by seeing, and even touching it. This is possible to the fact of a thing. For the fact of events, there could be difficulties of proving. The event if (direct) first witnesses no longer exist. Take the death of Julius Nyerere next 200 years; in such a case you are obliged to depend on reliable official documents (hospital report, state house report, death certificate) newspapers, diaries all of them are facts in their own right and thus can inform you objectively.

3.   Origin of Ideas

Origin of ideas is an old philosophical argument; since the time of Plato, Aristotle and their subsequent followers and other philosophers. Our interest here is not to trace what which philosopher said and what the other did not say.

Our stand and for the purpose of pragmatism is that every logical idea in the mind can be traceable to a substantial thing independent from that in the mind. Our ideas are the means through which we generate knowledge; they link us to facts in the world. You can be able to verify your ideas through the objects they represent in the world.

4.   Be Mindful of the Origins of Ideas

It is natural that most individuals like their ideas because they are products of our/their brains. It is necessary to note that though you own your ideas- their origin is independent of your mind; the ideas originate from things outside of your mind those include objective facts in the physical world,

This fact is important for it enables you understand that your ideas can be concretized in the real world and that their origin comes from there. When you intend to search for fact you should not simply rely on your ideas because those ones are only subjective facts; objective fact that you refer to or intend to establish is that found in the physical world that of which your ideas confirm with objects in the physical world.

5.   Relate Ideas to Facts

In the realm (sphere) of human knowledge there are three basic components; one is an objective fact (Example; a cup) two is the idea of a cup; three the word we apply to the idea, allowing us to communicate to other people (*Example in English, "cup"*) (McInerny, 2004), Refer to Plato and Aristotle on ideas. Everything on this example begins with the cup. If a real cup didn't exist then there wouldn't be an idea about them and there would be no word for that idea. Ideas are clear as much as they reflect objective reality in the world.

In relating our ideas in the mind and real entities in the physical world, there are simple and complex experiences. The correlation between the idea of a cup and a real cup is simple and indeed direct. The idea matches with only one entity called a cup in English.

The complex idea is when there is no single and simple correspondence between idea and entity. Let us take the idea of *development*. There is no direct correlation on the one to one basis – *development* entails many sources and facts that give meaning to the idea of development. Thus to understand your idea of development it must refer to what is common between you and others, the many facts that constitute to development. Therefore, as you develop your personal ideas make sure that they are known by others or you can explain, teach your ideas to others.

6.   Relate Words to Ideas

We have just seen the necessity of relating our ideas (*existing in the mind*) to facts (*existing in the physical world*). Ideas especially good and progressive ones are necessary for people's progress in the world; unfortunately so far it is not possible/ easy to communicate ideas from one mind to another. Ideas that are not communicable to others cannot be useful to society. They can be communicated through words; you have to look for the right word to clothe your idea and pass it on to others. The procedure of getting the right word for your idea is that of going to the source of your idea(s) the real entity in the physical world. This procedure applies to both simple and complex ideas.

7. Effective Communication

Effective communication makes the discussion of logic possible. Communication is possible through language. If you wish to communicate with others then you need to put, as we have shortly seen, your ideas into words. Putting ideas in words is not enough for finding truth which is the object of logic; several ideas and thus several words will lead into statement. Words are important as they represent our ideas; however, statements are the starting point of logic for it is only in statement that we can be able to establish truth or falsity of what we intend to communicate.

Communication alone is not enough to establish truth in our statement and communication in general, thus we need effective communication. Effective communication enables proper presentation of our ideas and thus your thinking can reach the targeted population and hence obtain your fulfillment in life. Effective communication is possible and can be attained through the following procedures:

i. Use Complete Sentences

Logic deals with a complete sentence in the form of a complete statement. Do not use phrases or clauses that are incomplete such as "The Prime Minister Mtwara", "Poverty in rural". When one hears these phrases will know that you intend to pass on some information but which in this case is incomplete. To be understood properly, you need to speak in complete sentences; The Prime Minister visited Mtwara region last week", "Tanzanian poverty is mainly found in the rural settings."

ii. Avoid Double Negatives

In English the double negative makes a sentence affirmative; for instance "it is not uncommon to meet with a rich man without formal education". This kind of sentence could cause confusion as it sounds negative where as in the real sense it is positive. Thus to avoid confusion simply say; "there are rich men without formal education"

iii.   Make your Talk Explicit

When passing information to the audiences do not assume the background is known to all; make it explicit. Pass all the information completely; it is better to pass too much information rather than passing too little.

iv.   Direct your Language to your Audience

When you have an opportunity to address an audience you have to know their education background at least the majority of them. If you are a medical doctor, you should not use the technical terms of your profession simply to impress people; use the right language depending on the type of audience.

8.   Be Careful with Vague Ambiguous Language

Vague means "not clear" a word could be used but readers or /and listeners may not understand what it is pointing at/ to consider the following statement: "they don't like such clothe". A response to the statement would be who are "they"? And what kind of "such clothe?" In that statement we are not sure what exactly is intended because we do not have clear information. To make it clearer replace the words that are unclear with what is clearer: "they" say "young people of this generation", "such clothe" – the clothe that elders put on in the 60's

Ambiguous means having more than one meaning and its content does not explicitly indicate which meaning it is intending. A sign at a parking site written: "Parking at owner's risk" could be understood in two different ways: the first meaning of *owner* could be:

1.   Owner of the premise
2.   Owner of the vehicle to be parked

Thus the right way to avoid ambiguous statement is to precise what we intend to say. Such as "Parking is at vehicle owner's risk" or "Parked vehicles are protected by the premise."

9. Avoid Evasive Language (being indirect)

It is important that you always use a direct language when addressing an audience that anyone paying reasonable attention would get the meaning. An evasive language has two problems that you need to avoid. The first one is that it can deceive your audience. The second is it could even be more harmful to those who use an evasive kind of language as it can distort the sense of reality.

Thus in order for you to avoid all kind of such problems and have your audience get the message that you intend then to grasp from you simply use a direct language.

10. Truth

The purpose of reasoning is to attain the truth of things. This is a hard task as truth can at times be a painful difficult endevour. However, failure to pursue truth would be unreasonable, since it is truth that gives meaning to all our activities. It would equally be unreasonable to think that truth is something to be pursued forever and never be attained, that would make our activities "purposeless" goalless and that would mean irrational of us (*human beings*) but we know that is not the case.

Truth has two forms; ontological truth and logical truth. Ontological truth is truth of existence (being in existence). A thing is ontologically true if it actually exists; that is it has real being. The book in your hand is ontologically true for it is really in existence.

Logical truth is the form of truth that logicians are mostly concerned with. Logical truth is the truth of statements. In the early pages of this chapter, we discussed about this truth of statement that it is obtained when there is conformity between idea(s) and the real thing in existence.

The Basic Principles of Logic

In the early pages of the book we defined logic as a science. Being a science it is led by principles. Any science is led by first principles that guide that kind of science. The first principles guiding logic are unique since they apply to other sciences too. Logic is guided by three principles which are also known as principles of human reasoning.

The First Principle: The Principle of Identity
It states that: *A thing is what it is* or *Each thing is identical with itself*

The Second Principle: The Principle of Excluded Middle
It states that: *For any proposition, either that proposition is true or its negation is true* or *There is no Middle State between Being and Non-being.* That is something either exists or it does not exist; there is no halfway point between the two cases.

The Third Principle:
The Principle of Non-Contradiction
It states that contradictory propositions cannot both be true in the same sense at the same time or *It is impossible for something both to be and not be at the same time and in the same respect*

Example:
   a. John Pombe Magufuli was a member of the Tanzanian parliament in 2010 -2015
   b. John Pombe Magufuli was not a member of the Tanzanian parliament in 2010 – 2015

Both of these statements cannot be true. If one is true, the other must be false, and vice versa. As for this case we know for sure that statement "a" is true, therefore, statement "b" is false.

An example of logical thinking

Complete the following sequence by writing the steps as required in logical thinking

   a.   14, 15, 17, 20, _

       1.   <u>Goal</u>:

Find the 5th number in the sequence

2.   <u>**Information**</u>:
   4 numbers of a sequence in ascending order

3.   <u>**Condition**</u>: We observe that
   14+1= 15, 15+2 = 17, 17+3 = 20

4.   <u>**Reasoning**</u>:
   We add 1 to the first number and get the second number
   14+1 = 15

   We add 2 to the second number and get the third number
   15+2 = 17

   We add 3 to the third number and get the fourth number
   17+3 = 20

   Therefore, we should add 4 to the fourth number to get the fifth number

5.   <u>**Solution**</u>: 20+4 = 24

To conclude bear this in mind that this logical thinking skill when mastered at the proper level, enables you as an individual to carry out your activities in a more serious, systematic and in an in-depth manner. It is at this juncture that as a scientist you could come up with a discovery, a new theory, or an innovation on how to do something in a completely different way in life; as an artist too you may come up with a novel way of approaching or operating things in life.

Further Readings

McInerny, D.Q. 2004. Being Logical A Guide to Good Thinking, Random House, New York

Powers, Melvin.2001. The Art of Dynamic Thinking: The Technique for Achieving Self-Confidence and Success. Better Yourself Books. Mumbai

Green, Robert. 2012. Mastery, Penguin Group. New York

CHAPTER FIVE

Thinking Critically

Critical thinking is a tool containing skills that have gained fame recently, otherwise in the past educators were mainly interested in teaching content of the different subjects (Fisher, 2013: Chaffee, 2012). There are many definitions for critical thinking: John Dewey (1859-1952) an American philosopher, psychologist and educator who is regarded as a "father" of modern critical thinking looks at critical thinking as an active process of which you think things through yourself, raise questions for yourself, find pertinent response yourself, make conclusion and judgment yourself rather than learning in a passive way from someone else. Robert Ennis (1927-) an important contributor to the development of modern critical thinking argues that critical thinking is reasonable, reflective thinking that is focused on deciding what to believe in or do (Fisher, 2013)

Critical Thinking is a skill enabling a person to think clearly and rationally while understanding the logical connection between ideas. It is a skill involving several other skills specifically reflective and independent thinking. Critical thinking aims at attaining the best possible outcome in any argument. It is also regarded as the ability to analyse information objectively and make reasoned judgment and decisions. In order to do so; it collects and assesses information from many different sources.

Moreover, critical thinking involves thinking for yourself by carefully examining the way that you make sense of the world. Practicing this approach in life is great aspect of being a mature human being (Chaffee, 2012). We human beings and you as a university student are able to think critically because of our natural human ability to reflect and think back on what we are thinking, feeling or doing. By reflecting on our thinking, we are able to find out the way our thinking operates hence we can learn how to think more critically and effectively (Fisher, 2013; Chaffee, 2012). This is an important point for you as a university student; developing a reflecting routine behaviour (thinking back) on what you are doing, feeling or thinking of operating. This should be your operating pattern even though you should always think, visualize what you intend to do before you actually do it. Thus as you do it then, you bring in the reflection pattern which is kind of evaluation; this evaluation should function in the same manner as what monitoring and evaluation does in a development project.

Characteristics of an Effective Critical Thinker
A critical thinker should behave in a particular way. As a critical thinker you have to cultivate certain characteristics that should be demonstrated in your dealings which could be a business meeting, individual work or a public community meeting. To become an effective critical thinker you have to be able to:

1. Listen carefully to the arguments and ideas of others
2. Comprehend the relations between ideas
3. Determine the importance and significance of arguments and ideas raised in a meeting
4. Identify, formulate and examine arguments
5. With the help of your logical skills you should be able to identify inconsistencies and mistakes in reasoning
6. Tackle a problem in a consistent and logical way
7. Ponder on your own assumptions, opinions, principles and values
8. Reflect on your own proposed argument and conclusion

How Can you Think Critically?
Critical thinking involves rigorous questioning of ideas and assumptions rather than simply accepting them at face value. Critical thinking intends to determine whether the ideas, arguments and findings represent the entire picture of the subject matter in question.

Start with Self-reasoning Skills
Thinking critically is associated with digestion of ideas, thoughts, and arguments. Digestion is done by reasoning; reasoning starts with ourselves. It entails;

i.   Having reasons for what we do and believe and being conscious of them;
ii.   Critical evaluation of our own deeds and beliefs;
iii. Ability to present to others the reasons for our deeds and beliefs

This may seem to be easy as often as many of us assume that we know what we believe in and why we do. Nevertheless, when we are asked to explain why what we believe in is true, it becomes apparent to us that we haven't thought thoroughly on what we have heard or seen but rather seems to be a point of view of just one side. It is thus necessary to examine the foundation of our own belief and reasoning for it is from that point that one begins to practice critical thinking (Cottrell, 2005).

Critical Examination of other's Reasoning
Critical reasoning normally considers other people's reasoning too. This requires the skills of understanding their argument, and skills of analyzing and evaluating it in detail. In summation form, critical analysis of other people's reasoning requires the following:

i.   Identifying their reasons and conclusions;
ii.   Analyzing how they reason to make an argument
iii. Examining whether their reasoning supports their conclusion;
iv.   Examining whether their reasoning is informed by reliable evidence; and
v.   Identifying mistakes in their reasoning (Cottrell, 2005).

A university student, according to the missions of many African universities, is supposed to be an individual who acquires skills to be able to solve some issues in his/her community through work as an employee. Thus you are expected to be critical enough at constructive issues and important arguments; however you are expected to carry out critical examination of different activities in a respective manner.

In order for you to be able to think critically you need to develop a number of skills such as observation, analysis, interpretation, evaluation, reflection, explanation, inference, problem solving and decision making. The aforementioned skills could be developed through learning of life skills that contain most or all of these tools you need for critical thinking and other skills are obtained when you learn research skills as a research student at the university level of your studies.

The skills mentioned above enable you to think critically; moreover, specifically you need to:

1. Think about an issue in an objective and critical way
2. Identify the different views that are in a relation to a particular issue
3. Assess a point of view to determine its validity or pertinence in the given context
4. Identify any weaknesses that are found in the argument
5. Give an organized reasoning and support an argument that you would like to make (needed skills)[20]

Why Should you Think Critically?

Thinking critically, combined with other skills, enables you arrive at truth. Truth or underlying truth of affairs is important for it helps you know things as they are in themselves. You get to know the reality of affairs when you know the naked truth that enable you in making informed decisions and judgments on whatever you do in life. Thinking critically enables you use philosophical tools of skepticism and doubt constructively so that you analyse what is before you. It helps you make better and more informed decisions about something

---

[20] https://www.skillsyouneed.com/learn/critical-thinking.html
(Obtained 10-10-2019)

whether it is true, effective and/or productive (Cottrell, 2005). An effective critical thinker becomes a good decision maker.

Decision making is an important quality of a leader in associations, in politics and in any other organizations for that matter. Decisions make things move faster in organizations and thus lead to people's progress and profit in case of business. When decisions are made they could be correct or wrong; if you asked for counsel on what you should do fast? I will tell you it is decision making fast that counts more important to me, if you make wrong decisions you will have time to correct it, whereas if you delayed too much in making decision, you will forgo or miss many opportunities that would contribute to people's progress. Moreover, as a university student you are expected to possess qualities, skills that, to some extent, will protect you from making silly mistakes when you make decisions. However, even what is called silly mistakes could turn into opportunity as you can learn from the same faults.

Critical thinking enables you gain skills that will inform you the noumena of things that is things as they are in themselves. Thus a keen critical thinker becomes a great and indeed effective leader because s/he makes informed decisions backed up by facts and thus leading to well-being of people. Take an example of business choice; when a person wants to choose a life career between two careers that attract an individual: Agri-business and IT business. For an effective leader –S/he will involve critical thinking. The person will analyse all/most businesses, see how they perform, examine their demands. Requirements, profits, how much a business will improve his and other people's living standards directly and or indirectly and above all a critical thinker will examine oneself to know where their talents apply best in between the two businesses. There could be several decisions made; take one business and concentrate only on that with all strength and energy or take both businesses and establish a company that houses both businesses look for talented individuals in those fields and perform well.

Precision is defined as accuracy and or freedom from error- this freedom from mistakes is brought about by critical thinking. When you start thinking critically you become more accurate and specific in finding out what is pertinent and what is not. The skills accompanying or brought about by critical thinking as we saw earlier are necessary and useful to solving problems, and management of project enabling accuracy to different parts of a project (Cottrell, 2005).

It is obvious that you possess some self-appraisal skills needed in everyday life. Nevertheless, as you advance in your studies or in your professional activities then you need to refine your critical thinking skills. Lack of self-consciousness and weak reasoning skills could lead you to weak self-appraisal and poor marks in academic performance. For university students there are remarques from their lecturers suggesting that some students fail to score higher marks because their assignments lack rigorous critical thinking. Critical thinking for you is necessary for it helps you explore deeper below the surface of the courses that you are studying. You can sharpen your critical skills through participation in critical debate, seminars, presentations or peer reviewed papers for publication (Fisher, 2013; Cottrell, 2005)

When the critical thinking skill is mastered at the proper level it enables you as an individual carry out your activities boldly in a more serious, systematic, and in an in-depth manner. It is at this juncture that as a scientist you could come up with a discovery, a new theory, or an innovation on how to do something differently as it has been done before; as an artist too you may come up with a novel way of approaching or operating things in life.

Further Readings

Cottrell, Stella.2005. Critical Thinking Skills: Developing Effective Analysis and Argument. Palgrave MacMillan. New York

Chaffee, John (2012) Thinking Critically, 10th Edition, Wadsworth, Boston

Fisher, Alec. 2013. Critical Thinking: An introduction 2nd Edition. Cambridge University Press. Cambridge

https://www.skillsyouneed.com/learn/critical-thinking.html

Green, Robert. 2012. Mastery, Penguin Group. New York

CHAPTER SIX

Thinking Strategically

"The greatest waste in the world is the difference between what we are and what we could become" Ben Herbster

This is yet another important and necessary skill needed by youth, university students, and any individual who wants to succeed in life. Strategic thinking is another title made up of thinking as a noun (gerund) and strategic as an adjective.

Thinking as defined earlier in other chapters is one of the mental activities; it is one among many activities of the brain which coordinates activities of all organs and systems in your body. Thus thinking is an action or means of using your mind to producing thoughts.

Strategy is the skill that enables an individual or organization to examine the current situation, organize the resources around and be able to move to the future with those resources. (Mckeown, 2014) a renowned strategist thinker himself defines strategy as being able to move from where you are to where you want to be. He argues that smart strategy is the shortest route to desirable ends with available means.

Strategy originates from the Greek word *strategos* meaning someone or a general who has an army to lead in war. The word was first used in Greece in 508 BC to describe the art of leadership demonstrated by ten generals who were in the war council of Athens. The generals developed competent leadership skills that achieved set objectives. They also developed different approaches to war and motivation skills to soldiers (Mckeown, 2014). Mckeonwn argues further that similar ideas about strategy were also developed by Sun Tzu in his book Art of War (200 BC). The book is still pertinent and sold today. The book outlines different principles that leaders may follow to win and achieve their goals.

Business strategy is relatively new as compared to war strategy, it became popular mainly after the Second World War; it is only then that books for guiding business leaders started appearing.

I compare strategic thinking with a mathematics problem of division. The problem of division requires a number of other skills apart from that of division itself; it requires multiplication, subtraction and even addition skills- I have observed that in my grade three son when solving his mathematics homework problems. This analogy with strategic thinking works too as strategic thinking requires a number of other skills such as critical thinking, independent thinking, logical thinking, creative thinking, and imagination (visualization). Strategic thinking deals with the manner in which people think about, examine, view and create the future for themselves and others.

How to Think Strategically?
Everyone and you included can train to become a strategic thinker. This skill is necessary as it helps you foresee your future and helps you attain it with the current available resources and means.

If you want to think strategically, as said already earlier, you have to learn a number of other skills that will accompany you in strategic thinking. You need to activate your abilities in: thinking independently, thinking logically, thinking critically, thinking creatively, and thinking analytically. Each of these skills empowers you in one area which helps you to think really strategically. As you think strategically you will need to bear in mind between two approaches in strategic thinking; analytical and creative strategies.

In analytical strategy you think strategically while analyzing your situation or the situation of your business or any other activities that you operate. Analytical is from analysis that is separating a whole into parts while studying each of them carefully all with the purpose of shaping your current situation. On the other hand, in creative strategy you make use of your imagination abilities, you foresee your future or that of your company after being informed by strategic analysis. Depending on your abilities you may decide to use one of the approaches or both of them.

Strategic thinking is necessary and indeed important, however, it is hard; for if it were easy then every individual and company would succeed, but they don't argues Richard Whittington in Mckeown 2014. The essential is to learn how to think better and do it differently according to your natural abilities. Despite the different approaches to strategic thinking what is important that you should know is that your decisions will involve risks because you are betting on a future that is uncertain and complex with preparations that are as well uncertain and complex. Some strategic preparations demand for long time, effort, and even pain before benefits come your way. However, it is important to keep in mind that no matter how strategic you are results will not necessarily happen the way you want them to happen, and thus you should join with smart strategists who know that events don't necessarily occur the way you planned and thus reaction may be as important as planning itself (Mckeown 2014).

In their book Strategic Thinking: A nine step approach to strategy and leadership for managers and marketers, Wootton & Horne (2010) present us with an approach that you can use to strategise in your businesses and any other endevours. They say it is important to think about what might have changed, be changing or will be changing in the areas that have direct connection with your business or your activities and those areas are those of technology, economy, markets, politics, laws, ethics, and society.

A Strategic Thinking Tool

A strategic thinking tool as developed by Wootton & Horner

	What is the likely impact on your organization in the following period			
	Medium Term		Long Term	
	Problem	Opportunity	Problem	Opportunity
Technology				
Economy				
Markets				
Politics				
Law				
Ethics				
Society				

Changes in Technology:
- How will improvements in communication methods change the way you work with your customers, suppliers and employees?
- How will you be affected by high speed broadband?
- How will you be affected by different technologies such as nanotechnology?

Changes in Economics:
- How would movements in key economic indicators affect you? Growth in unemployment, falling inflation, increasing imports, more graduates seeking for work
- Is your growth restricted by a shortage of thinking skills?

Changes in Market:
- How large is your market? How many competitors do you have, where are they?
- Do you require a great amount of capital to penetrate the market?
- How easy can a new entrant be able to find the initial capital?
- Does your business need particular channels of distribution? If so are they vulnerable to be controlled by a competitor?

- Does your organization provide services or goods that are unique? Could your customer obtain benefits they get from your product in another way?
- How easily could competitors copy what you do?

Changes in Politics:
- Is your company taking advantage of current taxation politics?
- What decisions are likely from existing or new governments worldwide?
- How could political changes in overseas countries have implications from your customer or for your suppliers?
- How could you be affected by a collapse of good governance in one of your markets eg. Collapse of law and order?

Changes in Law:
- How will your company be affected by changes in climate change regulations, employment law, health and safety legislation?
- Will regulatory bodies develop policies that affect you?

Changes in Ethics:
- Does your company look after people's health and welfare?
- Are you considering altering your sources of raw materials?
- Does your company recycle where possible?
- Does your company have a stress management policy?
- What pressure groups are interested in your business?
- Does your company promote fair treatment for all irrespective of colour, culture, religion, race, age, sexuality?

Changes in Society:
- Does your company involve employees and customers in decisions that affect them?
- What is the impact of new threats to health and wellbeing?

Moreover, the Harvard Business School presents a pattern that you can follow to learn how to think strategically; here are the six steps that you may follow to succeed in strategic thinking. They include the ability to: anticipate, challenge, interpret, decide, align, learn, consistence, agile.

Anticipate

As a strategic student, leader or individual you have to be vigilant on maximizing the ability to anticipate by constantly examining the surroundings for signals of change. To be able to do so you need to be connected with individuals, organisations, your stakeholders that will feed you with information needed in your field or in the market if you are on business–the connections will provide you with the data you need to anticipate results of the future.

Change

As a strategic thinker you need to question the state of affairs. You need to question your assumptions those of your colleagues and encourage for various opinion from stakeholders. When you carefully examine the issues at stake it is when you can be able to make a meaningful action. To arrive to that point demands for courage, open mind, perseverance and patience.

Interpret

As a good leader, good student you are expected to be able to get information from different services and be able to get sense out of it. No matter how ambiguous and complex the information is, you should be able to synthesize and interpret it so that it benefits your business/project.

Decide

Decision making is a quality indeed necessary for effective leaders and so it is an important and necessary tool for a strategic thinker. Fast decision making facilitates growth of a business or any enterprise if the decision is correctly made. To be sure of making correct information you need together all possible and necessary information for you to analyse, synthesize, interpret and make decision. As a strategic thinker you have to visualize the implication of your decisions in short and long terms phases.

Align

Alignment of all important stakeholders' views in the object you intend to implement is of paramount importance. These colleagues of yours should be able to see your vision, understand it get convinced and work with you to attain the goal of the project/ business. Definitely you need a strong team to be successful in business. Alignment of your stakeholders requires meeting with them in person, talking with them about your plans, make them understand the objectives/ goal of your business and work with them to success.

Learn

As a strategic thinker you need to be an open minded person and take learning as an important component of your business. Let your colleagues who are aligned in the vision of your business work freely take informed risks, work hard for success. When you and they fail take those failures seriously, draw learned lessons out of the failure. In fact, you need to establish a culture of documenting all failures; analyse them to find out the causes of failure and most important the lesson learned. The lesson learned should be shared amongst key team players (Schoemaker, et al.2019). Thus as s good strategic thinker you need to work diligently on the skills we have identified and explained above. You need to find out the weaknesses correct them and apply them for a successful business and you are ready for success.

Why Strategic Thinking?

Strategic thinking is a skill that enables an individual, business or company to foresee the shaping of the future; it is about how you can attain desirable ends with available means and resources at your disposal. It is as much about deciding what to do, where to go, why, when and how as about choosing what not to do. Yes, No. What if. Why not?

Strategic thinking has five basic questions from which others may emerge:

i.   Where are you?
ii.   Where do you want to go?
iii.   What changes do you have to make?
iv.   How should you make the changes?
v.   How should you measure progress?

When the strategic thinking skill is well mastered it enables you as an individual carry out your activities confidently in a more planned, strategic, and in an in-depth manner. It is at this juncture that as a scientist you could come up with a discovery, a new theory, or an invention on how to do things, businesses successfully and in completely different ways; and as an artist too you may come up with a novel way of approaching or operating things in life.

Further Readings

Mckeown, Max.2014. The Strategy book 2nd Edition, Pearson. London

Harvard Business Review Press (HBR). 2019. Guide to Thinking Strategically, Harvard Business School Publishing Corporation. Boston

Green, Robert. 2012. Mastery, Penguin Group. New York

Wootton, Simon and Horne, Terry. 2010. Strategic Thinking: A nine step approach to strategy and leadership for managers and marketers. 3rd Edition. Kogan Page Limited. London

CHAPTER SEVEN

Thinking Creatively

The subject above is composed of two realities: thinking and creativity. Creativity is from the verb "to create" that is making or enhancing something new to exist or come into existence. Creativity is a part of the mind and spirit that help us bring into existence, seemingly out of nothing, something useful and indeed significant. However, creativity starts with what exists already, thus creativity takes place when a thinker transforms an existing material into a new reality of greater value (Adair, 2007). Therefore, creativity is the ability to make something new.

Thinking is a mental activity that ponders and reflects on an issue keenly for a particular purpose mostly understanding it and thus facilitating decision making. Creative thinking is the ability to reflect, look at issues differently, and be able to find new ways of solving problems. Judkins (2015) argues that thinking creatively is not a professional activity but rather creative thinking is about creating yourself, creating a much better future and taking opportunities that right now you are missing them.

How do you Think Creatively?
There are different techniques that can enable you think creatively. Here we have a list which, however, we don't claim to be exhaustive: this one is given to help you activate your creative thinking ability if it has been in a slumber state.

Perform Different Tasks
Your brain can be activated to think creatively when you operate different tasks that are not in your area of expertise. When you work as an amateur and an unprofessional you become open to new ideas and

there you can do anything. At that level you do not know how that thing should be done, and you are not yet accustomed in a particular approach to do things. There is nothing "wrong" for you because you do not know what is "right" in that field (Judkins, 2015: skillsyouneed, n.d).

Avoid Becoming an Expert

It is important you avoid becoming an expert, authority or specialist if you wish to think creatively. I know this may sound strange because as we continue with the formal education especially the higher degrees the system "forces" you become an expert. There is nothing wrong with you becoming an expert but when it comes to creative thinking think as an unprofessional. As an expert you will simply be consulting your past experience, whatever worked for you in the past, you are likely to repeat it. When you become an authority then new ideas, new approaches become a threat to your expertise and so you are likely to block them out. The moment you do so you systematically, consciously or unconsciously prevent creativity in you (Judkins, 2015: Adair, 2007; skillsyouneed, n.d).

Switching Jobs

Switching jobs encourages creativity and innovation in your undertaking, business or organization. Spend time working on something important but not in your area of expertise; changing jobs "forces" you to look for new ways of doing things differently and in an unordinary ways (Judkins, 2015; skillsyouneed, n.d). This you can practice best when you finish your studies and start searching for a job at that moment you become open to any job that comes before you; it is a good opportunity for you to strengthen your creative abilities. Take such opportunities. The profession you have acquired through your studies will be applicable in different ways in other jobs and if you real wish to use it, you may still come back to it at the time you wish to.

Be Yourself

To become a creative thinker you do not need to imitate someone else; you have plenty of sources from where you can draw your ideas and insights for creativity. Make the most of your uniqueness. You can get ideas, inspiring thoughts from your childhood, teenage, schooling experiences. Those moments are rich and pregnant with insight for creativity. People search for originality elsewhere, forgetting that it is there within them; instead they are busy being someone else and thus limiting their originality and creativeness.

To be a successive creative thinker you have to know that it is alright to be yourself. All of us have our strength and weaknesses a creative thinker accepts them and uses both for originality. It is thus by being yourself that you maximize the opportunities of practicing creative thinking.

Why Thinking Creatively?
Creative thinking is a tool that improves life in an extraordinary way. It helps you find solution to problems facing your community. The major responsibility or role of education and more especially if that education is linked to university is to solve problems facing individuals (Mandalu, 2019). Education and/or knowledge has the task of improving lives by translating what is acquired through senses into real activities that help solve community problems.

It minimizes cost when solving problems in a community. A creative thinker uses the available resources to finding remedy of the current situation. A creative thinker with the help of other skills that you have learned in the previous chapters such as critical thinking and logical thinking employs their inborn abilities to bring about important solution facing a community, organization or any other entity. Since the thinker uses the available resources.

Creative thinking encourages the sharpening of other necessary skills you need in your daily practical life. Some of the skills include: imagination, originality, open-mindedness, risk taking and spontaneity. Imagination helps you become a creative person in the sense that you sharpen your ability in thinking and visualize new ideas, possibilities that could lead to that which has never existed before.

Imagination is well done when it works hand in hand with originality. You as an individual person are unique in the sense that there is no any other human being with capabilities that are only found in you. Thus employing your imagination abilities may lead to original ideas that never existed before.

Open-mindedness is the readiness to accept different possibilities when searching for solution to problems. This tool is essential for a creative thinker as s/he will be ready to welcome different possibilities and by so doing increase the chances to getting the required solution.

Risk taking in creative thinking is crucial as it calls upon daring into new ventures leaving behind the already established proceedings or solution. It is this tool that when it is accompanied with other skills seen above, it facilitates creative thinking leading to new ways of doing things, solving problems and completely original ways thus giving a fresh view of life.

To conclude the chapter, I would like to remind you that it is creative thinking that in most cases has defined eras in human history. Whenever human beings came up with a new way of doing things life on earth changed. When the early human being (Homo erectus) started walking upright it brought changes to his/her life, when he started using tools; it made life easier than before, the discovery of electricity, the invention of printing, the invention in telecommunication, the invention of internet and much more inventions and discoveries fall under this skill of creative thinking. Thus if you wish to live a meaningful and contributive life to your community of human beings then creative thinking is a tool that you need to embrace, nurture and sharpen it.

When the creative thinking skill is well mastered and combined with other discussed skills it enables you as an individual carry out your activities creatively in a more planned, systematic, and in an in-depth manner. It is at this juncture that as a scientist you may come up with discoveries, a new theory, or an invention on how to do things, businesses successfully and in completely novel ways; and as an artist too you may come up with much more original ways of approaching or operating things in life. To succeed in whatever you plan to do with your life is a decision lying in your hands.

Further Readings

Judkins, Rod.2015. The Art of Creative Thinking. Sceptre. London

Adair, John.2007. The art of creative thinking: how to develop your powers of innovation and creativity. Kogan Page Limited. London

Green, Robert. 2012. Mastery, Penguin Group. New York

CHAPTER EIGHT

Thinking Positively

Positive thinking, like other "thinkings" that we have already seen such as creative thinking, logical thinking, critical thinking, strategic thinking, and others, is a mental activity. It is an activity occurring in the mind. It occurs in our conscious mind and gets stored in the unconscious or subconscious mind.

Wilson (n, d) defines positive thinking as a mental attitude in which an individual anticipates hopes or waits for good and favourable thing(s) to happen to him/her. A positive mind hopes for happiness, health and happy ending in all undertakings. Positive thinking means approaching life tasks with a positive approach. It does not mean avoiding bad things, rather it extracts good sides of things even in bad situations, looking at the best sides of other individuals, and seeing yourself and your capabilities in a positive attitude (Powers, 2003). This condition could be your real situation at campus where you live and interact with all kind of individuals; people of different backgrounds, different value; both friends and those that you don't get along well with. It is in such a situation that you need to have positive thinking and affirm yourself before the colleagues you live with.

Thinking is a mental activity and often starts with self-talks. Self-talks are endless unspoken thoughts that could be positive or negative. These thoughts have different sources; some come from logical reasoning while others come from misconception due to lack of proper information (Mayo, n.d). If most of your thoughts are positive and behave in that manner then you become termed as an optimist, whereas if most of your thoughts are negative and behave in that manner you become a pessimist.

We human beings are said to have about 60,000 thoughts in a day of which most of them come and go so fast that we are not even aware of them (Wilson, n.d). Our thoughts are imprisoned in the Kantian category of time that is they stuck and divided in the times we experience: past, present and future.

Thoughts about the Past

Thinking about the past wastes a lot of our quality time. Most of the time when we think of the past it is about our past mistakes, sad moments, the decisions we made of which none of them we rectify as nobody can alter the past. The best we can do about our past through our thoughts (thinking) is to draw good lessons from our past experiences. It is thought much as 80 percent of our thoughts are about the past.

Thoughts about the Future

It is thought that another great share of our time is spent on thinking and worrying about the future. It is argued that about 15 percent of thoughts of an average person is spent on worrying about the future.

Thoughts about Present

From statistics, it is only 5 percent that is left for thinking of the present. The thoughts about the present are divided into positive, negative and necessary. From the 5 percent, positive thoughts account for only about 1 or 2 percent, the rest is left for the other two kinds of thoughts.

That is how the quality of thoughts of a human person including you looks like. Our life, love, peace, happiness, success depend very much on the quality of our thoughts. Thus success in life depends very much on your positive thoughts. Your positive thoughts relate or lead you to peace, affirmation, love, purity, happiness and success. While your negative thoughts direct you to feelings of anger, hatred, fear and all kind of feelings that pull you down. Whereas, necessary thoughts relate to daily activities such as your planning (Anthony, 2007)

How do You Think Positively?
You can think positively by doing certain acts and or by behaving in a certain manner that will see you develop your ability to positive thinking and develop a positive attitude.

Learn how to control your mental attitude; that is how and what you think about. Look at things from their positive side. You must fill your mind with positive thoughts all the time. Fill your mind with the thoughts of success, let your surrounding reflect too on the thoughts of success. To obtain all success and become a good positive thinker requires self-discipline and sense of purpose. Make sure that your purpose in life is clear in your mind and you respect and follow it.

Carry out examination of conscious every day. You may do it every evening before going to bed; this will help you evaluate your day. From your activities of the day check what you have done to contribute on your personal development. Investing in your self is indeed very crucial for you to be able to attain success in your life. When you examine your life through assessing your daily activities as suggests Socrates – then you are capable of seeing what you have been investing in yourself. Make sure that you do something for your personal growth every day; do not simply do the ordinary duties as tasked by your employer. Do something for yourself even if it is small – it will add up and become something big.

You must be optimistic at all times. Things may appear hard and difficult but you still have to be optimistic. You have to look at the positive side of things; always look at what is positive in a difficult situation that you are facing. The typical example to demonstrate the difference between these two individuals is that of a glass of water. The pessimist; a person filled with negative thoughts, a person who often discourages himself/herself, sees the glass of water as half empty while the optimist; a person who most often saturates his/her mind with positive thoughts, sees the glass of water is half full. A person with negative thoughts looks at difficulties as a problem to be avoided whereas a positive thinker sees an opportunity to create something good out of it.

Successful positive thinking needs a set goal in life. A successful positive thinker needs to have a direction of where s/he places her optimism. As a university student you have the task of studying, acquiring knowledge, acquiring skills such as independent thinking, logical thinking, critical thinking, analytical skills and much more. The university education in itself is not a goal; it is simply a stage in education where, if you are careful enough, you acquire some specialized skills. Since you have opted for the university path to attain life skills then you should be helped by those skills to attain your goal in life. The attitude of positive thinking and constancy on your goal in life makes you successful. In other words positive thinking is demonstrated on individuals with well-defined goals.

In life each one of us and you have the opportunity to succeed. However, you first of all need to know the universal laws, universal principles because life operates according to those principles. The principles are trustworthy, reliable and unchangeable. You can trust them and if you follow them; they will always give you the desired results. The universe forces or energies are neutral and give results to any person who applies them; it does not care whether you are tall, short, male or female. Your religion does not count for success if you do not apply the principles; it is necessary to say this as Mbiti puts it that an African is notoriously religious, when it comes to these energies what counts is how do you direct those forces to operate according to your thinking, ideas, dreams, goals and beliefs to obtain the results you want. And thus at this juncture positive thinking becomes indeed necessary for your success.

Your own word is a law in the universe and so you have to be careful of what you say about yourself. To be successful however, depends on your knowledge and application of the laws, in ignorance you cannot be or create what you want to. Cause and effect is a fundamental law to which other laws conform. The principle operates in such a way that the result equals to the cause. The cause is always an idea, thinking and /or belief. Therefore, your ideas will lead you to success or failure depending on the content of your ideas, thinking.

The law of cause and effect is neutral or impersonal. It does not depend on your religion, kindness, or any other great attributes that you possess; it only follows the rules, the logic. In that sense you might see kind, loving, pious. God fearing individuals but still live in poverty, simply because they are ignorant of the success principles in the universe (Anthony, 2007).

Why Should you Think Positively?
Positive thinking is a skill with lots of benefits to those who practice it. As a university student searching for skills, I think you have a moral obligation to acquire this skill as you are full of latent potential. Learn to think positively because there is so much that you can obtain through or extract from the skill.

When you master well the positive thinking skill and combine it with other acquired skills it enables you as an individual carry out your activities more positively, creatively in a more planned, systematic, and in an in-depth manner. It is at this juncture that as a scientist you may come up with discoveries, a new theory, or an invention on how to do things, businesses successfully and in completely novel ways; and as an artist too you may come up with much more original ways of approaching or operating things in life. To succeed in whatever you plan to do with your life is a decision lying in your hands; you only need to make that decision and get going.

Further Readings

Anthony, Robert.2007. Beyond Positive Thinking: A No nonsense for
    Getting The Results You want, Morgan James Publishing, New
    York

Wilson, Livi (n.d) Art of Positive Thinking, Scientist Demersal
    Fisheries Division, CMFRI

Green, Robert. 2012. Mastery, Penguin Group. New York

CHAPTER NINE

Thinking in Systems

Thinking is an important activity of the human brain. Thinking as we have already discussed in earlier chapters could be creative, leading to creativity and thus enabling innovation; finding solution to problems that have existed for ages. Thinking could be independent fortifying an individual's ability and consciousness which facilitates progress in life. Moreover, thinking could as well be strategic; a skill needed so much in organization, institutions and in any other form of gathering where a clear vision and focus are needed. It is through that same mental activity, thinking that we are able to simplify the hardship of life and improve the living standard of human beings.

Systems thinking or as I put it thinking in systems is an investigative tool for examining problems more completely and accurately before acting. It empowers us with better questions before making conclusions. It starts with observation of collected data to identify patterns of behaviour accrued overtime revealing to us the underlying structures that determine the data and pattern. By understanding and changing structures that do not operate well, we can increase choices and create more fulfilling, long-term solutions to chronic problems. The thinking in systems demands you to possess certain qualities: curiosity, kindness, clarity, choice and courage. Thinking in systems involves the readiness to view a situation as a whole, to realize that we are interrelated, to admit that there are multiple interventions to problems (Goodman, n.d).

A system is a purposeful collection of inter-related components that form a unified whole working together to achieve some common goal. Systems are made up of three parts: *elements*, *interconnections*, and a *function* or a *purpose* Function is used for non-human systems and purpose for human systems (Schuster, 2018; Meadows, 2008). Since you are university student then starting with an example of a university as system can help you understand better what a system looks like.

A university is a system and the elements (actors) include lecturers, students, principals, deans, secretaries, librarians, drivers, cooks, nurses, parents and counselor. The interconnections are the relationships between the elements, the university regulations, the time table and communications between all of the people at the University. The purpose of a University is to prepare students for a successful future; help them reach their full latent potential.

A football team is yet another example of a system: its elements include players, coach, playground, and a ball. Its interconnections are the football rules, coaches' strategies, and players' communications. The purpose of the team is to win matches, or make money, or get exercise or all of the mentioned purposes (Schuster, 2018, Meadows, 2008).

From the examples given above you can see that a system is seen as an entity made up of parts. Each of those parts is necessary and important, once a part ceases to exist, a system changes. Systems can change, seek goals, and repair injuries. Systems can be self-organizing, self-repairing depending on the kind of injuries. They are strong, and many tend to be evolutionary and thus out of one system a completely new system may arise (Meadows, 2008).

Elements in the systems are the most noticeable ones, interconnections and purposes are least conspicuous. While all of the parts are important and necessary because they work together, the elements are important but could easily be changed without much effect on the system. Interconnections between elements are necessary and could greatly affect a system once changed. And changing of the purpose has the greatest impact on the system as a whole (Schuster, 2018)

Thinking in systems therefore is the kind of mental activity that allows us to look at a complete picture of a whole all at once. We do not look at parts in a whole but rather we look at a complete and in fact the whole picture all at once and see how the members in a system interact with each other to reach their specific goal, their purpose of being, their raison d'être. If we interchange these two concepts *systems thinking* and *thinking in systems*; we shall then define thinking in systems as the study of complexity of the relationships and interactions among components of a system or it is a conscious thinking of the complexity of the relationships and interactions among components of a system. Thinking in systems is normally introduced with an expression "*the whole is more than the sum of its parts*" and this expression of togetherness resounds in an African saying: "*I am because we are.*"

How Do you Think in Systems?

On thinking, there is no one way that is the best of them all; you should take thinking as a tool box where there are different tools for different purposes. You can employ the different kinds of thinking to solve different problems facing our society depending on the situation you find yourself in.

We can shift from one kind of thinking to another such as from linear thinking to systems thinking. Linear thinking deals with symptoms whereas thinking in systems addresses the real problem. Thinking in systems addresses the real problem by careful analysis on the systems behavior patterns, elements, interconnections and purpose or function.

As a thinker in systems, you always have to bear in mind the three components: elements, interconnections and purpose or function. You have to know how they behave and relate with each other in a system so as to know how a system functions as you see it operating.

Moreover, you have to keep in mind that elements are the most visible components in a system; they are the doers or actors while they are important and so much conspicuous components in a system; they can easily be replaced and the system may continue to function at times better or worse than before.

Interconnections, while not so much visible, are necessary components in a system; they deal with the sensitive part of the flow of information that directs the elements how to operate, relate and even behave in a system. They cannot easily be replaced; once they are changed the system will cease to function properly as it has been programmed or designed to function.

Purpose or function; this is component that defines how a system should operate this is the raison d'être of a system. Once this is changed, the system becomes something different; it ceases to be what it is, it becomes something different.

While thinking in systems is useful for most or all complex problems, it is more appropriate for a problem that has been solved but the problem keeps on coming back time and again. It is at that moment that you can introduce thinking in systems as an option to be preferred. You should begin by asking different questions to get different answers when you begin your systems thinking analysis, it is possible that the data and information that you have is just a tip of the iceberg

Be sure to speak with everyone in the system so that all of their viewpoints are represented. It is only by listening to all perspectives that you truly get to the heart of the problem. Once you have gathered all information think of informing all the members about the nature of collected information so that you can be able to move forward together with them with the same understanding.

As you begin the analysis, keep the parts of the analysis simple, small and digestible. Feedback from systems can provide us with invaluable learning opportunities. We should always seek to gain knowledge from every life experience. It will serve to improve our analytical skills, and sense of awareness (Schuster, 2018), making us better equipped to make evaluations, judgments and decisions. Remember life is the total sum of the choices (decisions) you make every day in life.

Why Thinking in Systems?
Thinking in system is necessary and a great approach to solving human problems because it takes the approach of wholeness and not from the

sectorial point of view. Today big challenges cut across human and natural systems; to address them it requires multiple interdependent variables that change over time, and indicating future changes which are critically important and yet complex to predict. These features are some of the essential characteristics of systems that call upon thinking in systems, an essential tool to students and future workforce, to address complexity of systems to solve community issues such as unemployment, poverty, food resources, conflicts, climate change, and diseases[21].

Thinking in systems is an essential tool to you because as an individual you need to stock stories of success in life; this tool enables you tackle complex issues and give solution to your community. As a leader in your company, institution, community, you need to be resourceful and render yourself useful to the community specifically where you live and in general to the whole human community.

Being able to solve complex problems in your community, country and even at the international level, gives you recognition, sense of satisfaction, sense of importance, and definitely it raises your self-esteem. Solving community problems improves your income and certainly history books guarantee records of your contribution to the well-being of the human race beyond borders of your country.

When the thinking in system skill is well mastered and combined with other discussed skills it enables you as an individual carry out your activities from a holistic point of view, and in an in-depth manner. It is at this juncture that as a scientist you may come up with discoveries, a new theory, or an invention on how to do things, businesses successfully and in completely novel ways; and as an artist too you may come up with much more original ways of approaching or operating things in life. To succeed in whatever you plan to do with your life is a decision in your hands. Mastery of thinking in systems could also be

---

[21]https://serc.carleton.edu/integrate/teaching_materials/systems_what.htmlRetrieved on 02nd February, 2020

showing you your real purpose in life; a thing that many individuals fail to create in life and thus live aimlessly and without sense of purpose.

Further Readings

Meadows, H. Donella.2008. Thinking in Systems, Earthscan, London

Schuster, Steve. 2018. The Art of Thinking in Systems: Improve your logic, think more critically, and use Proven Systems to Solve your Problems. Strategic Planning for everyday Life

Green, Robert. 2012. Mastery, Penguin Group. New York

CHAPTER TEN

The Purpose of Life

I conceive life and here referring to as a life of a living being and specifically a human person, as the totality of all the time and space from the first heartbeat to the last one. The question here is when does the first heartbeat begin? On conception; when a sperm fertilizes an ovary? Or when exactly does it commence? When fertilization takes place a new being, a new life comes into existence. However, at that particular point the new being needs great deal of time to be full conscious of itself. Thus, one may argue that life begins when one becomes conscious of oneself. The statement begs for a question; does consciousness occur at the same time to all individuals? There could emerge several questions of the same nature; however, science can tell us better about this; otherwise, it is food for thought.

Purpose of life is the reason of being alive; the essence of being in existence for a being; it is the raison d'être of an individual. It is that which an individual means to do, get or be. That means each and every human person including you is here on earth for a specific purpose. Every individual is unique and thus his/her raison d'être is also unique different from everybody else's. The task before you is to know what your purpose in life is. Even as you are breathing right now within you there is a purpose for you being alive; you may or may not know about it, all the same there is still a purpose for you being there. What is that purpose? That is your life time task which if you want to live a meaningful life then you should know and live it before you die. However from the purpose of life subject a necessary and huge question imposes itself: is the purpose of life discovered or created?

Is the Purpose of Life Discovered or Invented?
From the description above you see that a purpose of life is necessary for it gives you direction and guidance as to how you could plan,

organize and execute your daily activities in life so as to bring meaning in your life. In his article "Meaning in Life: Discovered or Created", Baird (1985), presents a good analysis on whether a meaning in life is discovered or invented. A number of philosophers, in the article, describe life and consequently the purpose of life in a very pessimistic manner that if you are not careful enough and if you have not developed well your critical, analytical and independent thinking skills, you could easily join them as a pessimist. Jean-Paul Sartre (A French philosopher 1905 – 1980) argues "All existing beings are born for no reason, continue through weakness and die by accident..." Bertrand Russell (A British philosopher 1872-1970) argues that "All the labours of ages, all devotion, all inspirations, and all the noonday brightness of human genius are destined to extinction..."

Contemplating to such philosophies, you might feel like losing your mind. However, the skills you learnt earlier should be pertinent tools to empower you with the strength and skills you need. And we can now move on with our key question in this section. Is purpose in life discovered or invented (created)? When you take discovering for an answer to our question it appears that the purpose of life exists somewhere out there and that it is waiting for an individual to unveil it, to discover it. Whereas inventing or creating has a different connotation for it implies responsibility upon individuals; that is, you as a person have the task of designing your purpose to guide your life. Science and religion tell us that a human person is superior to all other living beings because of his highly developed brain which coordinates all activities in the body. It is your brain that makes you function as an intelligent being. That is to say, you can observe, learn, process issues within you and make decisions. Thus, it is your intelligence that helps you or should help you invent your purpose in life.

When I reason on whether the purpose of life is invented or created, there are many individuals out there who argue that the purpose of life is discovered. It is already there, you simply have to uncover it, and you can lead your life happily. I personally don't subscribe to this school of thought or understanding simply because it denies a person of their freedom which is embedded in that highly human developed brain.

The human brain operates through its principles in spite of depending on the data it is fed with such as upbringing, environment, beliefs, peer-influence and the like.

How to Create your Life Purpose

Creating one's purpose in life and living it is such a great act of a human person being full alive and responsible in life. Moreover, it is an act that renders fulfillment in a life of a human person of which you too partake and have the right to experience it. In order for you to create your purpose in life, the sense of consciousness is necessary; you have to be conscious of yourself. You have to know who you are, what your capabilities are, what your limitations are, what you like and dislike. In a nutshell you have to go back to chapter two where you discovered your own self – self-awareness. Becoming conscious of oneself helps us realise our natural gifts that we are born with as they are coded in our genetic makeup; these gifts and talents should inform you on what and how to craft your purpose in life.

Jack Canfield (1944) is an accomplished American author, motivational speaker, corporate trainer, and entrepreneur. I concur with him on his tips on how to invent one's purpose in life. However, I differ with him and other coaches of success on the manner the purpose in life is obtained. For him, the purpose in life is discovered; that is, it is somewhere out there waiting for you to unveil it. Whereas for me, the purpose in life is invented; you work for it; you design and create it in the way you want it to be as informed by your talents, gifts and interests. Here are suggestions and/or guidelines that could help you in inventing your purpose in life.

1. **Examine the Things You Love to do and What Comes Easily to You**

Every individual is unique and endowed with gifts and talents; you need to interrogate yourself and investigate on what you do so as to find out your talents. Practicing your talents will lead you and contribute to your journey to attaining happiness, which according to Socrates, is the purpose of life. Talent, according to Dubois, 2015, is that gift, an activity that an individual does or that which comes easily to him/her and make him/her find joy and happiness when doing it. Happiness is the climax of satisfaction from what you do in life, and so if you create a meaningful purpose in life, you will be a happy person.

Any talent requires practice to attain mastery, and for talent to be seen, felt or to be heard, it must impact people's lives (Dubois, 2015). *Practice makes it perfect* thus goes an English adage. Thus, you need to practice on what comes easily to you to attain the level of mastery and satisfaction.

To be able to identify your talents, look at what you have done spontaneously in the past and others praised you for that. That phenomenon could have happened during your childhood, adolescence; when you were doing a certain field work or apprenticeship, or even today in your daily activities (Dubois, 2015). Recall what you have done with easy and naturally without much effort and start from there. It does not matter how small it is or insignificant you might think it is; it is already a good starting point.

2.   **Employ a Maieutic Approach**

Socrates was fond of using a question and answer approach, dialogue in dialectic form (thesis, anti-thesis and synthesis) to attain the right answer. Canfield proposes a schema of asking yourself two questions; one, ask yourself: what two qualities do you feel happy to express to the world? It could be happiness, joy, love etc and for Canfield he says his two qualities he likes expressing are joy and love.

The second question that you should ask yourself is; what two ways do you enjoy expressing those qualities. Depending on your real life experience, it could be anything such as teaching, facilitating, coaching, inspiring, encouraging, empowering individual, caring for the sick, preaching etc. And his two ways of expressing the qualities are inspiring and empowering people.

Canfield inspires people by narrating moving stories in his seminars and by writing them in his books. He empowers the people by teaching them powerful success strategies that could be applied by his students and readers in real life.

3. Invent your Life Purpose

When you have done the two first steps above, it is now time to come up with your life purpose statement. As Canfield suggests, write your life statement based on your point of view. The statement should be according to your conviction such as all individuals in the world should live according to their full potential and value. Now combine all the three steps to come up with what would be your life purpose statement. Canfield displays his life purpose statement as inspiring and empowering people to live their highest vision in a context of love and joy.

4. Listen to your Inner Voice

Every individual has within themselves an inner voice which guides them on how to go about in what they do. This inner voice in you operates as a Global Positioning System (GPS) that operates in your vehicle or in your smart phone.

When you intend to go somewhere, you indicate your current location; once the GPS determines your location, then, through the signals it receives from satellites it directs you how you could get to your destination.

Canfield suggests that all you have to do is to decide where exactly you want to go by clarifying your vision, position yourself towards your destination by setting your goals. Then, visualize and affirm what you want to become, in the meantime put in action some real activities. Even as you set your goal(s), affirm and visualize yourself doing those activities; you still need to do some real work with your hands.

5. Be Clear on your Life Purpose

A score of motivational speakers and writers have insisted on this. Keep your vision or life purpose clear and keep your mind constantly focused on it; follow your inner voice for it knows what is right and what isn't.

Socrates advised youth that *an unexamined life is not worth living.* Therefore, take time to reflect, meditate honestly on your life, your current situation and what you want to do with your life. Remember through your intelligence; thanks to your human highly developed brain; you can create what you want.

What is your current financial status? How is your marriage relationship? How are your other relationships behaving? How is your psychological life now? How is your health? When you have meditated about your current status, the next step is to think of where you would want to be.

The time for imagination and positive thinking comes in now; if you were in your perfect world right now, how would your life look like? What kind of work would you be doing? Where would you be living? What life style would you be having? Continuing with this exercise will be sending signals to your subconscious mind which will drive your dreams and life purpose to reality.

6. Carry out a Passion Test

The passions you have in life help you live your life enthusiastically. They are, to life, what spices are to food; they make the food more palatable. Moreover, they help you discover your talents and help you in creating your life purpose.

Canfield proposes a passion test as developed by Chris and Janet Attwood. He argues that the test presents you with 15 blank spaces that you have to fill in. The test starts with the statement; *"When my life is ideal, I'm ..."* in order for the test to make sense, the response that you fill in the blank space must be a verb. Here is an example as performed by Canfield:

- My life is ideal when I'm being of service to massive numbers of people.
- My life is ideal when I'm helping people with their vision.
- My life is ideal when I'm speaking to large groups

- My life is ideal when I'm being part of a spiritual leaders network.
- My life is ideal when I'm creating core group of ongoing trainers who feel identified with my organization.

From the example above you can now come up with your own statements that help you have an ideal life. Make 15 statements and identify the top 5 to make comparison and draw the most important ones that make sense in your life.

Once you have identified your top 5 important passion, then examine if you live your life according to your passion and if those passions help you invent your purpose in life. Another example from Canfield serves the purpose here:

> "A life goal would be, when I'm helping people live their vision I'm giving at least 20 workshops a year for at least 10000 people, and from each event people bring feedback saying you've really empowered me to live my vision"

When this test or any other test of this kind helps you discover your passions, and helps you figure out how your life would look like when you put into practice the findings of your tests; you can now create action plans to convent your dreams into authentic reality.

7. Recall your Happy Moments

Recalling of your joy and happy moments is yet another effective tool in identifying your strength and helps you create your life purpose. Set aside 30 minutes and make a list of those great moments. In fact this is the same message we get in ***"count your blessings; name them one by one…x2"***.

For Canfield, who in this section we take him as a case study, some of his strong moments were as follows: when he was a patrol leader in the

Boys Scouts, when he was a summer camp counselor, when he was a leader in his college years, when he was conducting workshops and training, and when he was travelling. What about you? What are your strong moments? Count and/or name them.

When you are done with the naming and or counting of your strong moments you are now ready to draw a pattern among all those moments. That is in what situations did the happy moments occur to you? In the case of Canfield those moments occurred to him when he was teaching, and when he was inspiring and empowering people to reach their dreams and to have more love, joy, fulfillment, satisfaction and much wealth in their lives.

Since you now know that joy and happiness are part of your inner voice and guidance system informing you when you are on the right track. When you do this exercise faithfully it can help you determine and guide you in designing and creating your life purpose.

8.   Learning From others to Create your Life Purpose

Human beings are unique, gifted differently and yet they have the capability of learning from others. Let us take a case study from Canfield as he interacted with one of his many students.

One of his coaching students had hard time in creating his life purpose through the above approach and so he gave him a different option to realise the task. The student was asked to reflect on his life and answer the following question which I suggest that you too dear reader should also personalize it "When have I felt most fulfilled?" The student came up with different answers that occurred in different occasions.

Canfield and his student realized that for all three answers the common feature that came out was the sense of freedom that the coaching student lived and experienced in those moments. Furthermore, Canfield realized that all happy moments of his students were not related to his profession; further analysis revealed that the coaching student was so much absorbed in his work that he forgot himself, and thus by doing so he was dying in himself. Through that experience the student discovered himself - "found himself", he has learnt to set enough time for his work and for himself; and this has helped him create his life purpose and forges ahead happily. And you too can do it!

9. Align Your Life Purpose with your Passions and Talents

We have learnt that through the gift of rationality we are capable of crafting our life purpose. We are capable of creating our life purpose through the help of our talents and passions.

Our talents and passions are within us and these are the ones that help us craft (our) your life purpose. That being the case, I urge you to create your life purpose, with the help of the steps above, in line with your talents and passions in you.

Once you decide what your life purpose is then you organize all activities in line with your life purpose. Do activities that lead you towards your life purpose; and thus, that being the case – your life purpose should help you choose a profession of your choice.

10. Live According to your Real Life Purpose

When you are satisfied with what you have created as your true life purpose, you don't have to repair the whole of your life all at once. Instead take your time to align your activities step by step (Canfield, n.d).

As you align your activities towards your life purpose, pay more attention to the feedback from those around you, your products and your feelings too.

Time to Succeed

As an individual you have dreams, and you have been advised to dream big time and again, and so now it is time to act upon your plans. To encourage you act on your dreams, I suggest you interrogate yourself the questions that are presented to us by a number of success coaches and motivational speakers including Myles, Tony Robinson, Canfield, Les Brown.

- Who are you?
- Right now, are you where you wanted to be?
- Have you fulfilled all you thought you would by now?
- Are you delighted with your life style, travels, and leisure you have always thought of?
- Do you want to have a more rewarding profession?
- Could your relationship be deeper, more rewarding and more meaningful?

If you have not excelled in the above aspects and those related - keep courage you still have the opportunity to do so and you can do it again and again.

It is my hope the book has shed some light on important matters of your life, and that these pages could be useful to you. If they are well read and put into practice they could change your life in ways that you have never thought of. The decision to change your life and succeed in life is in your hands; it is upon you to take the decision and move on in a purposive, fulfilled, and contributive life.

Further Readings

Baird, M. Robert. 1985. Meaning in Life: Discovered or Created?
     Journal of Religion and Health. Vol.24 No,2 pp117-124

Dubois, Thierry. 2015. Le Livre Pour Découvrir Vos Talents. Eyrolles,
     Paris
George, Archimandrite. 2006. Theosis: The True Purpose of Human
     Life. Holy Monastery of Saint Gregorios. Mount Athos

Leider, J Richard. 2004. The Power of Purpose: Creating Meaning in
     your Life and work, Berrett-Koehler Publishers, Inc. California

Millman, Dan.1993. The Life You were born to Live: A guide to
     finding your Life Purpose. H.J Kramer Inc. California

Warren, Rick. 2002. The Purpose Driven Life. Zondervan. Michigan

BIBLIOGRAPHY

Adair, John.2007. The Art of Creative Thinking: how to develop your powers of innovation and creativity. Kogan Page Limited. London

Angus, M. Rachel & Larson, W. Reed. 2011. *Adolescents' Development of Skills for Agency in youth Programs: Learning to Think Strategically.* Child Development, January/ February, Volume 82, Number 1, Page 277-294

Anthony, Robert.2007. Beyond Positive Thinking: A No nonsense for Getting The Results You want. Morgan James Publishing. New York

Baird, M. Robert. 1985. *Meaning in Life: Discovered or Created?* Journal of Religion and Health. Vol. 24 No,2 pp117-124

Chaffee, John (2012) Thinking Critically, 10th Edition, Wadsworth, Boston

Chen, Xiao –Ping. 2008. *Independent Thinking: A path to Outstanding Schorlarship.* Management and Organization Review 4:3 337-348, University of Washington

Cloete Nico and Maasen Peter. 2015. Roles of Universities and the African context

Cloete, Nico, Maassen Peter and Pillay Pundy.2015. Higher Education and National Development. International Encyclopedia: meanings and purposes of Higher Education

Cottrell, Stella.2005. Critical Thinking Skills: Developing Effective Analysis and Argument. Palgrave MacMillan. New York

De Ridder – Symoens (ed).2003. A History of the University in Europe, volume I Universities in the Middle Ages Cambridge University Press, Cambridge

Dubois, Thierry. 2015. Le Livre Pour Découvrir Vos Talents. Eyrolles. Paris

Fisher, Alec. 2013. Critical Thinking: An introduction 2nd Edition. Cambridge University Press. Cambridge

Gardner, Howard. 1985. Frame of Mind: The Theory of Multiple Intelligences: The Basic Book. New York

Green, Robert. 2012. Mastery, Penguin Group. New York

Goodman, Michael. (n.d) Systems Thinking: what, why, when, where and how? At https://thesystemsthinker.com/systems-thinking-what-why-when-where-and-how/ Retrieved on 21-02-2020

Going Global. 2014. Can Higher education solve Africa's job crisis? Understanding graduate employability in sub Saharan Africa. British Council

Harvard Business Review Press (HBR). 2019. Guide to Thinking Strategically. Harvard Business School Publishing Corporation. Boston

Judkins, Rod.2015. The Art of Creative Thinking. Sceptre. London

Leider J. Richard. 2004. The Power of Purpose. Berrett-Koehler Publishers, Inc. San Francisco

Mandalu, Martin. 2019. The Hidden Wealth of Tanzania. Niim Printing. Dar es Salaam

Mckeown, Max.2014. The Strategy book 2nd Edition, Pearson. London

McInerny, D.Q. 2004. Being Logical A Guide to Good Thinking, Random House, New York

Meadows, H. Donella.2008. Thinking in Systems. Earthscan. London

Mwita, Kelvin. 2018. Tanzania Employability: Perception of Human Resource Management Practitioners

Oketch Moses, McCowan Tristan, and Schendel Rebecca.2014. The impact of Tertiary Education on Development. A rigorous Literature Review. Department of International Development. UK

Pelikan, Jaroslav.1992. The Idea of the University: A Reexamination. Yale University. New Haven

Powers, Melvin.2001. The Art of Dynamic Thinking: The
        Technique for Achieving Self-Confidence and
        Success. Better Yourself Books. Mumbai

Schoemaker, Paul. J.H; Krupp, Steve & Howland,
        Samantha. Strategic Leadership: the Essential Skills
        in Harvard

Business Review Press (HBR). 2019. Guide to Thinking
        Strategically. Harvard Business School Publishing
        Corporation. Boston

Schuster, Steve. 2018. The Art of Thinking in Systems:
        Improve your logic, think more critically, and use
        Proven Systems to Solve your Problems. Strategic
        Planning for everyday Life

Scott. C. John.2006. The Mission of the Universities:
        Medieval to Post Modern Transformations. The journal of
        Higher Education, vol.77.no.1

Ukleja, Mick and Lorber, L. Robert. 2009. Who are you what
        do you want? Penguine Group, New York

Wilson, Livi (n.d) Art of Positive Thinking, Scientist
        Demersal Fisheries Division, CMFRI

Wootton, Simon and Horne, Terry. 2010. Strategic Thinking:
        A nine step approach to strategy and leadership for
        managers and marketers. 3rd Edition. Kogan Page
        Limited. London